T5-DHA-668

BEGONIAS
AS HOUSE PLANTS

BEGONIAS
AS HOUSE PLANTS

JACK KRAMER

Drawings by Andrew Roy Addkison

VAN NOSTRAND REINHOLD COMPANY

NEW YORK   CINCINNATI   ATLANTA   DALLAS   SAN FRANCISCO
LONDON   TORONTO   MELBOURNE

Copyright © 1976 by Litton Educational Publishing, Inc.
Library of Congress Catalog Card Number 76-11114
ISBN 0-442-24517-3

Originally published in 1967 as a hard cover book by E. P. Dutton & Co. Inc.
under the title: BEGONIAS—Indoors and Out.

All rights reserved. No part of this work covered by the copyright hereon
may be reproduced or used in any form or by any means—graphic, electronic,
or mechanical, including photocopying, recording, taping, or information
storage and retrieval systems—without written permission of the publisher.

PRINTED IN THE UNITED STATES OF AMERICA

Published in 1976 by Van Nostrand Reinhold Company
A division of Litton Educational Publishing, Inc.
450 West 33rd Street, New York, N.Y. 10001

Van Nostrand Reinhold Limited
1410 Birchmount Road, Scarborough, Ontario M1P 2E7, Canada

Van Nostrand Reinhold Australia Pty. Limited
17 Queen Street, Mitcham, Victoria 3132, Australia

Van Nostrand Reinhold Company Limited
Molly Millars Lane, Wokingham, Berkshire, England

16   15   14   13   12   11   10   9   8   7   6   5   4   3   2   1

CONTENTS

AUTHOR'S NOTE   10

PREFACE: THE DEPENDABLE BEGONIAS   11

1. FOR VARIETY, GROW BEGONIAS   13
   Foliage   14
   Flowers   14
   Classification   14
   Time of Bloom   15

2. STARTING A BEGONIA COLLECTION   17
   Selection   18
   Where to Grow Plants   18
   Species, Hybrids, and Cultivars   19

3. BASIC CULTURE   21
   Light   21
   Soil   21
   Containers   23
   How to Water   25
   Fertilizing   26
   Temperature and Humidity   27
   Repotting   27
   Pruning and Resting   28
   Pests and Diseases   29

4. PROPAGATION OF BEGONIAS   34
   Equipment   34
   Seed   35
   Stem Cuttings   36
   Leaf Cuttings   37
   Rhizome Cuttings   37
   Heel Cuttings   38
   How to Hybridize Begonias   38

5. BEGONIAS INDOORS   41
   Plant Room   42
   In Greenhouse   43
   Gift Begonias   44
   Bonsai and Tree Form   45
   Begonias in Terrariums   46

6. BEGONIAS OUTDOORS   48
   Begonias in the Landscape   49
   Climate and Begonias   51
   Outdoors in Containers   52
   Tuberous Begonias   54
   How to Grow Them   54
   Tuberous Begonia Flower Forms   56
   Tuberous Begonia Species   60
   Propagation of Tuberous Begonias   61
   In Garden Beds   61

7. THREE HUNDRED BEAUTIFUL BEGONIAS FOR YOU   63
   Semperflorens Begonias   63
   Hairy-leaved Begonias   65
   Angel Wing and Other Fibrous Begonias   70
   Rhizomatous Begonias   82
   Rex Begonias   92
   Miniature Begonias   96
   Basket Begonias   104
   Winter-flowering Tuberous Begonias   109
   Calla-lily Begonias   111

8. BEGONIAS FOR SHOW   113
   Societies, Shows, and Magazines   113
   Exhibiting Begonias   114
   Photographing Begonias   116

APPENDIX   118
   Where to Buy Begonias   118
   Shipping Plants   119
   Begonias with Small Leaves   119
   Begonias with Large Leaves   120
   Begonias for Foliage   120
   Begonias for Flower   120
   Begonias for Scent   120
   Begonias for Sun   120
   Begonias for Warm Locations   121
   Begonias for Cool Locations   121

BIBLIOGRAPHY   122

INDEX   123

)

LIST OF ILLUSTRATIONS

Photographs

(The photographs appearing on pages 57 and 59 are by Joyce R. Wilson; the balance are courtesy of Vetterle & Reinelt.)

Page 57, Ruffled Camellia
Page 57, Double Picotee
Page 59, Hanging type tuberous begonia
Page 69, 'Viaude'
Page 69, 'Wooly Bear'
Page 75, 'Orange Parade'
Page 75, 'Brookes'
Page 79, *B. schmidtiana*
Page 81, 'Catalina'
Page 84, 'Bunchi'
Page 85, 'Erythrophylla'
Page 88, 'Maphil'
Page 90, 'Illustrata'
Page 91, 'Spaulding'
Page 91, 'Speculata'
Page 95, Specimen Rex plants
Page 99, 'Chantilly Lace'
Page 100, *B. dregei*
Page 100, *B. foliosa*
Page 101, 'Lulandi'

Page 103, 'Ivy Ever'
Page 107, 'Elsie M. Frey'

Drawings

Page 67, *B. luxurians*
Page 68, *B. venosa*
Page 72, *B. coccinea*
Page 72, 'Grey Feather'
Page 76, 'Corbeille de Feu'
Page 76, *B. kellermanni*
Page 78, *B. parilis*
Page 78, *B. sceptrum*
Page 80, *B. valdensium*
Page 81, *B. lubbersi*
Page 85, 'Erythrophylla'
Page 87, *B. heracleifolia*
Page 87, *B. imperialis* 'Otto Forster'
Page 88, *B. purpurea*
Page 90, *B. dayi*
Page 91, 'Ricky Minter'
Page 95, 'Merry Christmas'
Page 102, *B. rotundifolia*
Page 108, 'Limminghei'
Page 109, 'President Carnot'
Page 110, 'Emily Clibran'

AUTHOR'S NOTE

Writing a garden book is never lonely work. There are many people I meet along the way who generously contribute information. I am especially grateful to Martha Van Ness of Pacifica, California, for her patient answering of many horticultural questions. I offer my special thanks to Mr. and Mrs. Carl Meyer of San Bruno, California, for allowing me to photograph begonias in their home and, later, for subsequent conversations about begonias. Grateful thanks are also due to Pat Antonelli of Antonelli Brothers in Santa Cruz for making photos available and for allowing me to roam their greenhouses. Thanks, too, to the American Begonia Society for answering my many queries and for their excellent monthly Bulletin. And I am sincerely grateful to my photographer, Joyce R. Wilson, who patiently shot and reshot begonias for me, and to my illustrator, Andrew R. Addkison, who contributed such fine line drawings for the book.

Of course, the biggest thanks go to the begonias. They have made many gray mornings bright for me, and have made possible this effort.

PREFACE:
THE DEPENDABLE BEGONIAS

It's not necessary to bestow accolades upon begonias. They are well-tested house plants that have weathered the years and are still popular. It is a horticultural fact that begonias grow and bloom well in the home. Although new plants come and go, the begonia lives on as a dependable indoor decoration. It is a versatile plant that can be grown with only a little sun and without pampering. And there are begonias for all types of growing, indoors and out.

To describe the thousands of begonias available today, together with their culture, would do little to acquaint the indoor gardener with the limitless possibilities of begonias. Rather, I shall discuss the most desirable ones I have grown. Some are selected for flowers, others for foliage. The purpose of this book is to cover fully my best begonias, indoors and out, rather than to cast a hurried glance over the whole family.

My notes on culture are not meant to be rules, only suggestions. The treatment outlined has worked for me under my conditions, and I hope it will work for you. Under your conditions, some modifications may be necessary. Your common sense plus my suggestions, however, should add up to successful begonia culture.

✸   ✸   ✸

Early in 1965 I moved from my Chicago apartment to Mill Valley, California. With me, I brought about 200 begonia plants, and lost only a few of them in the transition—further indication of their durability. In Chicago my begonias were grown mainly indoors, some outside in summer. Here they grow in an enclosed garden room, as well as in a patio, in the open garden, and on a deck, some staying outdoors all year.

This book is a compilation of my experience over the years in growing these plants under various conditions—a composite of my adventures with the amenable and colorful begonia.

JACK KRAMER

Mill Valley
California

1 FOR VARIETY, GROW BEGONIAS

Begonias are versatile plants. There are small ones to brighten a windowsill, medium and tall growers that make an ordinary planter a showpiece, and large branching species to decorate the corner of a room. Majestic giants are also available if you have room for them. There are the compact Rexes with fantastic leaf coloring and the everblooming Semperflorens and Angel Wings that continually brighten windows with their bloom. The trailing begonias with cascades of flowers are dramatic in any situation. As for tuberous begonias, they offer glorious color for the outdoor garden.

Because begonias are so varied in leaf form and flower color, they make splendid plants to decorate the home. The low growers like 'Leo C. Shippy' and 'Skeezar' are typical of plants with leaves that crown the pot. They look handsome on a coffee table. The Angel Wings are stunning when used as vertical accent against white walls; and a large Rhizomatous begonia, lush and healthy, is attractive for a table in an entry. A row of miniatures is bright and colorful at a bathroom window. Pots of flowering Semperflorens anyplace in the house make winter mornings cheerful. Bushy begonias like *B. boweri* and *B. imperialis* 'Otto Forster' are handsome for planting boxes; and for hanging baskets, what plant can surpass the popular 'Limminghei'?

Large-leaved begonias like 'Ricky Minter' and *B. ricinifolia* are especially good as accent plants in a special container. Begonias are excellent for spot decoration, but be sure, after a week or so, to replace them at windows so they can regain their strength. Some begonias are climbers, others creepers, and some grow into small trees. Is it any wonder that begonias are so popular? The choice for flowers, foliage, size, or type seems limitless.

FOLIAGE

No plant family has foliage more varied in color, shape, and texture. Well-grown plants resemble brilliant oil paintings. Leaves can be as small as a thumbnail, like those of the miniature 'China Doll,' or as large as the drum top of 'Ricky Minter.' Some are ruffled and scalloped like *B. manicata;* many are round and open-faced or in the shape of a lance. There are even some with feathery foliage.

Colors are wildly brilliant or subdued with a silver, bronze, or gold overlay. Leaves feel like silk or velvet or taffeta. Some are iridescent, and covered with minute hairs that glimmer in light. Others are slick and multicolored.

FLOWERS

The flowers of begonias usually grow in branching clusters, upright or pendent. *B. mazae* and 'Immense' produce airy tall sprays of blossoms. Others, like 'Orange Rubra' and 'Lucerna,' have colorful hanging inflorescence. Semperflorens begonias are bushy, and bloom throughout the year.

Flowers vary in size from insignificant to pretty and delicate to large and handsome. Some are brilliant red or orange; others are a subdued pink or off-white. In most cases, bracts match the color of the bloom. Begonias are generous with flowers, and a dozen different kinds bring color to the window garden all year.

CLASSIFICATION

Most authorities classify begonias according to root structure. For years, there were four groups: bulbous, rhizomatous, tuberous, and fibrous. In time these categories proved inadequate, for many plants fell into two groups and some fit none of them. A newer classification specifies eight, sometimes nine, groups, and these simplify identification. Mailorder companies usually list begonias as:

Semperflorens	Rhizomatous
Hairy-leaved (Hirsute)	Rex
Angel Wing	Miniature
Miscellaneous Fibrous Rooted	Tuberous
Basket	

TIME OF BLOOM

Begonias are desirable as house plants because so many of them bloom almost year round with average light and some care. Semperflorens plants are a veritable rainbow of color all summer. The Angel Wings are laden with bloom from March to May. Some Rhizomatous types have late-winter bloom from December to February; others are at peak of flower production in May and April. In the Hirsute group there are plants for fall, others for summer display. For Christmas and Easter there are colorful *Cheimanthas*, welcome additions to any room in the house. And for outdoor summer show, tuberous begonias are king.

Most of the year my plant room holds blooming begonias; I am rarely without something in flower. If you choose wisely, you too can have this flower pageant at your windows from spring to winter.

Here is a selection of some favorite flowering begonias:

SPRING

'Bunchi'	*B. heracleifolia*
B. convolvulacea	'Phyllomaniaca'
B. conchaefolia	'Margaritae'
B. decora	

SUMMER

B. acuminata
'Corallina'
B. goegoensis
B. hydrocotylifolia

B. luxurians
B. nitida
B. venosa

AUTUMN

'Alleryi'
'Corbeille de Feu'
B. foliosa

B. fuchsiodes
B. incana
B. maculata

WINTER

'Catalina'
B. cathayana
'Elsie M. Frey'

B. griffithi
'Limminghei'
'Weltoniensis'

2 STARTING A
BEGONIA COLLECTION

Mail-order houses and trading among hobbyists are the best sources of begonias. Plants are described in the catalogs of specialists, and shipment is fast, usually taking a week. Each species or cultivar is properly labeled and comes in a peat or plastic starter pot. I order most of my plants early in spring or fall, when it is safe to ship them and when they will have time to become established in good weather. In summer, excessive heat can ruin a shipment. Winter orders are generally at the customer's own risk. I exchange a great many plants with other hobbyists. This gives me the chance to find species not usually available, and I enjoy making new friends this way.

If you want mature plants, query your nearest mail-order house. Sometimes they are available, sometimes not. A selected list of suppliers is included at the end of this book.

Because there are so many classes of begonias and only so much growing space in the home, you may want to limit your indoor begonias to one group. I am always thrilled when I find an enthusiast with a specialized collection, perhaps only the choicest Angel Wings.

There are advantages to growing one type. Thus, all Angel Wings want sunshine and the same amount of moisture and warmth. Caring for plants is simplified. I have never been able to pass up a begonia of any kind, but I do try to group them to facilitate care.

SELECTION

Begonias are not miracle plants. All of them take some time, some effort, and some genuine interest to grow successfully. But some are easier to handle than others, more dependable to bloom. Through the years the dependable ones have become the popular begonias, the backbone of a good collection.

As a group, the Hirsutes and Rhizomatous kinds are the easiest to grow at home. They do not mind adverse conditions, and several of them tolerate less humidity than do other begonias. Angel Wings, too, are usually good house plants. Although Rex begonias require more humidity and shade than other kinds, there are some that can be grown successfully indoors. Here are begonias from several groups that I recommend for your first selection:

'Alleryi'	*B. foliosa*
'Alpha Gere'	*B. heracleifolia*
B. boweri	'Limminghei'
'Can Can'	'Mrs. Fred D. Scripps'
'China Doll'	'Ricinifolia'
'Ellen Dee'	'Weltoniensis'
'Erythrophylla'	

WHERE TO GROW PLANTS

Where there is light, there is an area in which to grow begonias. A place near a window is always a good location. My miniatures are sill-residents, a cheerful sight against the glass on winter mornings. Angel Wings and larger branching kinds are best grown in a garden or plant room where there is more space for them. Basket begonias are charming at any window in the house.

Rex begonias revel in a semishady humid location. A floor planter with a bed of gravel is a perfect place for them.

Leaves reach up to the window, where changing light on the foliage makes a kaleidoscope of color. Or try small plants of Rex begonias in a terrarium at a north window; they will grow lavishly.

If your growing area must be away from a window, the Rhizomatous begonias are best for you. They tolerate adverse conditions better than most plants, and can live a long time without a great deal of natural light. Hirsutes, too, sometimes defy cultural rules and thrive for many months on a coffee table or in other interior areas.

Sometimes I start my own tuberous begonias; sometimes I buy them already started; but I always grow them outdoors. I have never tried to grow them inside all year, but I am told that this is possible under fluorescent lights and with a little extra attention. Certainly, the magnificent flowers are worth every effort.

In plant room or sun porch or garden room, at bay window or any window, in bathroom or bedroom, in baskets hanging from the ceiling—in every place and any place—begonias are a delight.

Species, Hybrids, and Cultivars

There are 1,500 species in the Begoniaceae, and countless hybrids and cultivars. Sometimes "hybrid" is used interchangeably with "cultivar." A species is a wild begonia grown in nature; a natural hybrid is a cross between two species. A true cultivar is a plant that exists only under cultivated conditions and is propagated by seed or cuttings. In this book the names of species are italicized, cultivars are capitalized and enclosed with single quotation marks, following the rules of international nomenclature.

Because all begonias are interesting, I grow all types. Species are not difficult to handle if you know their habitat, the geographical location from which they come. Explore that area in books. Once you know the climate in which a plant grows naturally, you are on your way to proper culture for that plant. Guesswork is eliminated. For example, *B. evansiana* comes from China and Japan, where there are defined seasons, and records indicate hardiness to 35 F., and bloom period between June and October. *B. venosa* is from Brazil, where seasons are the opposite of ours and where there is no rainfall for months, an indication that the plant needs less water at one time of the year, and possibly goes dormant.

On the whole, cultivars are more robust than species, and are usually bred to excel in a specific trait—leaf form, abundant bloom, or heat resistance. When you buy an unfamiliar begonia, find out all you can about it. If it is a hybrid, make a record of the parents if you can. If it is a species, try to discover its country of origin.

What species lack in flower and form, they make up for in being unusual and so perhaps more interesting. *B. foliosa* looks like a fern; *B. alnifolia* suggests the beech tree; and 'Crestabruchi' resembles a head of lettuce.

3 *BASIC CULTURE*

Begonias are mainly from Brazil, Mexico, and Africa—parts of the world with diversified climates. Although reputedly easy to grow, they still need care. We cannot duplicate their natural conditions in our home, but we can—with good culture—help them to grow into handsome, lavish plants.

LIGHT

Some begonias thrive at sunny south windows, others in bright light, and some need semishade. Although begonias are often considered shade plants, this does not mean that they will grow and bloom in a dim hallway. In fact, many begonias want all possible sunshine, especially in winter. In summer some protection against noonday sun is necessary, though, except in the South, a screen usually suffices.

Try to turn your plants once a week so that all the leaves get light and growth is uniform. Keep them near windows where light is bright for maximum growth; paint your room off-white to reflect more light. Dark walls absorb light.

SOIL

Except for carbon, all nutrients are drawn in from the soil through the roots. Thus, having a good potting mix is a head start in successful begonia growing. Nitrogen promotes good leaf growth. Phosphoric acid is for root development, potash for strength; a good mix contains iron, manganese, calcium, and other elements as well. A sprinkling of bonemeal can always be added to promote flower production.

There are many recipes for a potting soil for begonias. The type of mix to use depends greatly on how you grow your plants and where you live. While it is true that begonias will grow in any soil—good, bad, or indifferent—for a length of time, they will not prosper and become specimen plants. To do well, they must have the right kind of soil, with adequate nutrients.

For many years I used soil bought by the bushel from a local nursery, and while my plants grew reasonably well, they did not really thrive. I started mixing my own soil for begonias, and the results were gratifying. The soil formulas I suggest have worked for me under my conditions. You may have to add to them or take away ingredients from them for your own individual conditions.

FOR RHIZOMATOUS BEGONIAS

3 parts loam
1 part coarse sand
1 part rotted leaf mold
bonemeal
charcoal

FOR FIBROUS BEGONIAS

3 parts loam
2 parts peat moss (optional)
1 part coarse leaf mold
1 part manure
1 part sand
bonemeal
charcoal

FOR REX BEGONIAS

2 parts coarse leaf mold
1 part top soil
1 part sand or pumice
charcoal

Commercial packaged soils are also available for planting, but I have never been successful using these mixes. I don't know exactly what the media contain, and while I know they are reasonably good for some begonias, they do not furnish the necessary nutrients for other begonias. They are also quite costly if a large quantity is needed.

CONTAINERS

Today there are so many different kinds of containers that you are sure to find some that will be attractive for your rooms. Although I grow most of my plants in standard clay pots, I like a few decorative containers for accent through the house.

Ceramic or glazed containers come in many sizes and shapes and an infinite variety of colors and textures. You can put the clay pot inside the glazed container or pot directly in these tubs. But since the decorative containers usually do not have drainage holes, be sure to pot plants carefully. Use a layer of lava stone as a drainage bed and place some charcoal chunks on the bottom to keep soil sweet. And buy a wood or metal or clay base to elevate the container above table or floor. Cork mats are also useful in preventing stains.

The unglazed tub or pot is off-white, high-fired to a smooth finish, and sufficiently porous for plant health, since it allows moisture to evaporate slowly through the walls. Glazed containers do not afford as good evaporation, but they are still fine for most begonias plants. Many are handsomely designed and come in a variety of colors. As for shapes, you will find deep cylinders, squat tubs, tapered and pedestal forms, concave and convex urns, and wall-bracket bowls.

For tall Angel Wing begonias you might like the deep cylinders; they are in good proportion to the height of the plants. Round squat tubs are best for Rhizomatous types. A special large container is always effective on the floor in an entry hall or in a room corner.

Standard clay pots are at last available in various shapes from 3 inches to 24 inches in diameter. The rimless flared-lip or Italian pot is simple in shape, and most attractive. Three-legged pots are also available; Rex begonias look elegant in them. And a group of plants always makes a better display than a single one.

Permanent redwood planters are attractive. You can use them on a window ledge or as a room divider. Inside the planters you will need metal bins. These containers work best for Hirsute and Rhizomatous begonias. Even in subdued light, and watered only once a week, the plants stay handsome for many months.

Concrete tubs, soy kegs, washtubs, and sawed-off barrels are best used outside and are discussed in Chapter 6.

The pot size you need depends on your plant size. With few exceptions—and these are noted in the plant descriptions—Rex begonias need medium-size pots and Semperflorens begonias, smaller ones. Mature plants of Angel Wing and other branching begonias need large pots. Rhizomatous kinds like to be crowded, and will grow better that way.

Always soak new pots for a few hours; otherwise, they will absorb the moisture that is necessary for the plant.

Sometimes the begonias you buy arrive in peat pots, also called starter pots. These are containers made of peat and wood fiber, usually treated with nutrients. They are available in sizes from 1½ inches to 4 inches in diameter and in a molded unit of 6 to 12 small trays. You plant begonia, pot and all; even when repotting, you don't take the plant out of the container. A peat pot has the advantage, then, of saving

the plant the shock of transplanting. And it furnishes nutrients for the young plant, for it becomes part of the growing
medium. I have used these starter pots for begonias with
good results. Some growers say that peat moss is acid and
therefore harmful to begonias, but I have not found this to be
true.

Many times, though, begonias are shipped in cardboard
wrappings; don't confuse these with starter peat pots. The
cardboard *should* be removed before potting the plant.

How to Water

It is true that overwatering kills begonias, but if all other
cultural conditions are good—soil, potting, light—a thorough
soaking followed by a drying out before watering the soil
again seems the best procedure. The roots have time to absorb all moisture, and if they are somewhat dry for a day,
there is little harm done. When to water depends on many
variables: weather, pot size, individual location. But there
are still some general rules that can be applied.

Large pots of soil hold moisture longer than small ones.
You need to water specimen begonias in 10- and 12-inch pots
only once a week in winter; twice a week in early spring;
three times a week in summer. In fall, go back to the twice-
a-week schedule. Begonias in 4- or 5- or 6-inch pots need
more care. In summer, water them daily. The rest of the year,
water about three times a week unless there is an unusually
gray period (then once a week).

Some of the old-fashioned methods of determining when a
plants needs water are still good: Feel the soil; if it is dry
and crumbly, water. Lift the pot; dry ones weigh less than
moist ones. Tap the side of a clay pot; if it has a hollow ring,
water the plant.

When you water begonias, really wet the soil until it becomes uniformly moist; then roots reach out and grow. Root
development is hampered if only one section of the soil is

moistened. If partial watering continues, roots stop growing and, of course, the plant dies.

Don't apply cold water; it shocks plants. I have a pail of water standing overnight for use in the morning, and I try to water my plants in the early morning hours and not at night when respiration is slow. Tap water is usually all right, for it rarely contains minerals harmful to begonias, but artificially softened water should be avoided. It is harmful to plants. Of course, rainwater is best of all.

FERTILIZING

Indoors, potted begonias require feeding, for repeated watering washes away nutrients. Fertilizer properly given is beneficial: it produces healthy begonias with strong leaf color and fine bloom. Administered recklessly, fertilizer is harmful if not fatal. Too much plant food locks the elements in the soil—it acts like a roadblock—and, ironically, the plant starves in the midst of plenty. Moderation is the rule. I use a 10-10-5 commercial soluble fertilizer, applying half the dosage recommended on the package label.

Fertilize plants when they are actively growing, usually in spring and summer. In cold weather, when some begonias are dormant, feed them only about every six weeks. Use Atlas Fish Emulsion in summer, once every two weeks, not at all the rest of the year. And every month flood your begonias with a strong hose spray to leach out chemicals that have accumulated in the soil. This is important and should be done religiously.

Do not feed freshly potted begonias because there are enough nutrients in new soil to sustain the plants for some time, and do not feed ailing plants. The roots are not ready to absorb the nutrients. Although foliar feeding—applying food to the leaves with a spray—is widely practiced, I have not found it satisfactory for begonias. Too many Rex and Hirsute types resent lingering moisture on leaves.

TEMPERATURE AND HUMIDITY

Begonias readily adjust to varying temperatures. Most of them are comfortable if you are, and average home conditions of 60 to 68 F. at night in winter, and 72 to 80 F. during the day are fine. As in Nature, a drop of 10 or 15 degrees in late evening is beneficial. Of course, some begonias prefer coolness and others warmth; this is discussed with each plant group.

Rex and Angel Wing begonias revel in humidity. Rhizomatous and Semperflorens types are not so demanding. Humidity makes plants grow well. Although some begonias get along with low humidity (20 percent), the majority need additional moisture in the air. A hygrometer in the growing area will indicate the exact percentage of moisture in the air. Less than 20 percent dries out furniture, sinuses—and plants. I try to maintain 50 percent humidity, which is ideal for most begonias.

Space humidifiers and misting can be used to add moisture to the air. By growing begonias together in groups you can create humidity too. Another successful method is to fill a window planter with a 2-inch bed of gravel. Keep the pebbles wet but not saturated; place pots on, not in, the moist stones.

If you mist your begonias, do so on bright days only. Spray the area around the plant, not the foliage. Wet leaves and dark days are an invitation to fungus disease.

House plants need a fresh-air atmosphere. I keep some windows partially open near, not in, the growing area most of the year. A small electric fan operating at slow speed also helps to circulate the air.

REPOTTING

When unpacked, begonias that have been in closed containers for several days are shocked by bright light. Do not immediately put them in sun. Wait three or four days before placing them at windows. A few days after that, they can be repotted.

To repot, put small pieces of pots (shards) over the drainage hole of a clean container; add a few chunks of charcoal to keep the soil sweet. Fill the bottom of the pot with enough soil for a footing and place the plant in the center of the pot and pour soil in and around the roots. Shake the container occasionally to settle the soil and fill it to within a half inch of the rim. Do not pot a begonia tightly. Water thoroughly and place the plant in a warm semishaded spot for a few days. Feed only when the plant starts to show new growth.

I do not follow a schedule for repotting. As a rule, spring is the best time, but, when convenient, I have planted in summer and fall without harm to the plants. My system is simple: when roots grow through the drainage hole or the soil looks soggy or when a plant is neither growing nor dying, I repot it.

To remove a mature begonia from a container, turn the pot upside down, grip the stem of the plant and the top of the soil with your fingers, and tap the pot rim with a hammer. Gently tease the plant loose and remove the old soil and crock from the root's network.

When repotting Rhizomatous begonias, do not cover the creeping rhizome with soil. This causes rot. Allow it to remain on top of the soil with the growing tip away from the pot's side.

PRUNING AND RESTING

Keep your plants looking nice. Cut off faded flowers and imperfect leaves; dust foliage. To encourage branching, pinch out tip growth. Tall begonias need staking and mature plants occasional pruning to keep them attractive. Do not be afraid to cut off stray branches and remove old, woody growth to give new shoots a chance to develop. Train your plant to grow into neat form. Angel Wing begonias need severe pruning after flowering. Semperflorens kinds must also be thinned at the base to promote bloom and more beautiful flowers. Trailing begonias are benefited if they are cut back; flowering tuberous kinds should be pinched to encourage branching before flower buds form.

Too little attention is given to plant dormancy. As noted earlier, in dull winter weather many begonias rest. This occurs in some groups, and then again might happen only to certain plants in other groups. So, when a healthy plant slows up and drops leaves, don't get panicky. Let it rest; water lightly and omit fertilizer. Chances are, it will spring to life at the first sign of warm weather. Rex begonias are famous for this behavior; do not let them fool you and do not try to force them to grow. Keep soil somewhat wet, and wait for signs of new growth. A period of rest is natural in the life cycle of many plants.

Pests and Diseases

Years ago I was constantly battling insects in my plant room. No sooner did I get rid of one pest than I had some other plague. It was a one-man war, and like all gardeners I tolerated it because I love plants. Today, I spend only a few hours a year combating pests. New insecticides have made indoor gardening the joy it should be. Begonias and other plants will always be bothered by some insects, but preventive measures go a long way in keeping plants free of pests and disease.

Keeping the growing area clean helps to keep your begonias healthy. Get rid of rotted leaves and flowers, and always work with clean tools and pots.

When you buy begonias from a grower you do not know, inspect and isolate the plants for about a week in an unheated place until you are sure they are pest-free.

If you grow many plants, spray their area with an all-purpose insecticide—I use Malathion—every month. Isolate any suspected plants—those with limp growth or any that appear sickly. Don't crowd plants. Give each one ample room so that air can circulate around it.

If a few plants are attacked by insects, try spraying them heavily with water or dunking each plant in a bucket of water. But if the infestation is heavy, you will need to use an insecticide. There are dozens of them available to help you help your plants. Some come in powdered form for dusting, others in liquids for spraying. Some are for outdoor gardens, others for inside the house. Make your selection carefully. A miticide won't cure disease, and the spray that kills mealybugs won't necessarily kill scale insects. So be sure you know the pest you are fighting before you buy insecticides. Then follow the package directions carefully; above all, protect children and pets from danger, storing all products out of their reach.

Although some growers have used the powdered forms on begonias, I find these insecticides can be harmful to hairy-leaved kinds. I mainly use liquid insecticides.

Commercial sprayers for insecticides are sold at nurseries; choose one that is convenient for you and the number of plants you grow. The Ortho Spray-ette comes in 2- or 4- or 6-gallon capacity. It attaches to your garden hose and has an "off and on" device. If your insecticide calls for 1 teaspoon to a gallon of water, merely fill the sprayer with water to the corresponding 1-gallon level, and add the insecticide. Detailed instructions are stenciled on the bottle.

If you have only a few plants, you might want to use a general household aerosol bomb. These push-button cans, though expensive, are convenient. Read labels carefully, and be sure the product you buy will kill the insect that has attacked your plants.

When using sprays, apply them steadily over, under, and around the leaves, flowers, and stems. Make sure the mist penetrates the foliage. Do not spray at close range; the recommended distance is 12 to 14 inches from the plant.

Here are some insecticides I keep in my garden medicine cabinet, ready at all times, but, hopefully, infrequently used:

Chlordane . . . . .Best for controlling ants.

Malathion . . . . .A good general spray for all sucking insects.

Dimite . . . . .Effective against red spider.

SuperCide . . . . Another good all-purpose spray for sucking insects.

Fermate and Captan . . . . .Fungicides for disease.

Sodium Selenate . . . . Effective against nematodes.

Cygon 2 E and Scope . . . . . . New systemic insecticides worth their weight in gold. One application protects plants for six months.

Bug-Getta . . . . .Kills snails and slugs overnight.

Diseases

Botrytis: Fungus causing gray fluffy mold on stems and leaves. Thrives on decayed foliage and flowers; germinates quickly in stale air and high humidity. CONTROL: Remove debris from growing area and avoid misting plants for at least a week. Put victims where there is good air circulation and brightness. Use Captan.

Mildew: Fungus that thrives in high humidity and cold. Causes pale spots on leaves. Attacks primarily Rex and tuberous begonias. CONTROL: Move plants to airy place. Apply Captan or Fermate.

Stem and root rot: Bacteria in debris on soil causes brown mold on stems. Tubers become soft; rhizomes, watery and rotted. Plant collapses. CONTROL: Gather and burn infected plants.

Leaf spot: Bacteria that thrive in excessive heat and humidity cause yellow circles on leaf surfaces. CONTROL: Isolate plants and cut off infected parts; then place plants in an airy spot.

PESTS

Aphids: Plant lice, usually tiny green, sometimes red or black, that suck juices from new growth, causing leaves to curl and eventually die. CONTROL: If a few plants are infested, try to flush out insects with water. Many plants require Malathion.

Mealybugs: White cottony sucking insects that gather in colonies in leaf axils and on undersides of leaves, resulting in slow death of plant. CONTROL: Malathion. Repeat 4 times at 1-week intervals to catch hatching eggs.

Red spiders: Diminutive mites usually red, sometimes brown, almost impossible to see. The little demons gather on lower sides of leaves in fine cobwebs and suck the cell sap from the plant. CONTROL: Dimite. Repeat 3 times at weekly intervals.

White flies: Sucking insects that cluster under leaves and cause foliage to turn yellow. CONTROL: Malathion.

Scale insects: Flat red or brown hard-shelled insects. Suck vital plant juices and can do considerable harm if not detected early. CONTROL: Malathion.

Slugs and snails: Slow-moving insects that feed at night on the foliage. CONTROL: Insecticide containing methaldehyde. Bug-Getta works wonders overnight, but you must dispose of shells in the morning.

Thrips: Small gray or black flying insects that cause brown or silver blotches under leaves. CONTROL: Cygon 2 E or Scope.

Ants: Do not attack begonias but reportedly carry disease from one plant to another. CONTROL: Chlordane.

Root nematodes: Microscopic parasites that cause root knots, swellings at the base of the stem or below the surface of the soil, causing begonias to be stunted. If severe, it can kill plant. CONTROL: sodium selenate.

Repeated applications of insecticides are usually needed to eradicate pests. Apply at the number of intervals recommended on the package.

4 PROPAGATION OF BEGONIAS

A time comes when every indoor gardener wants to increase his begonia collection. There is a prize plant to be shared or you want more of a special favorite. Besides, your own plants, like your own children, are always the best.

The American Begonia Society offers seeds of hard-to-get varieties, and catalogs list a representative selection. New begonias can be grown by: sowing seed, tip cuttings, stem cuttings, leaf cuttings, rhizome cuttings, and dividing old plants and tubers.

EQUIPMENT

A propagating box takes up little space, is easy to put together, and has many uses. You can germinate seeds in it, root cuttings, or let it be a temporary shelter for new arrivals. Making a propagating case is easy. You can use redwood or your grocer's empty fruit box. If possible, get a box approximately 16 by 20 inches and about 4 inches deep. Fruit boxes come in this size and are easy to handle. Empty wooden window glass boxes are good too. If there are no slits in the bottom, bore a few holes to permit water to escape. Have window glass cut for the sides of the box; your local glass shop can do this for you. Tack a ¼-inch molding around the bottom of the box, allowing a ⅛-inch space to slide the glass in place. Hold together the glass sides at the corners with masking tape. Have another piece of glass cut as a top for the case.

Plastic refrigerator dishes, glass casseroles, and small aquariums are also suitable as propagating cases.

Put a 2-inch layer of moist propagating mix in the bottom of the chosen container. Commercial packaged vermiculite is good for seeds. If vermiculite is not available, use a half-peat and half-sand mix or a combination of leaf mold, peat, and sand. Some growers swear by milled sphagnum moss. There are countless media for germinating seeds.

SEED

Sowing seed is interesting and exciting, though sometimes tricky and exacting. Still, it gives you many plants at little cost, and quite often is the only way to get a prize species. Be sure all materials used in the propagating case are clean and that the planting medium is sterile. Don't take chances with damping off—a fungus disease that can ruin seedlings quickly.

There are low-cost heating coils available that plug into ordinary electrical outlets to provide bottom heat for propagating cases. This heating method speeds seed germination appreciably. However, I find that by placing the case on top of a refrigerator or on two bricks on a radiator I get free bottom heat for the seeds. Try it; it works fine.

Scatter the seeds evenly and sparingly on a vermiculite-and-sand mix in a shallow aquarium. Put a piece of glass over the top of the case and place it in a warm (78 F.) semishady corner. The condensation on the glass will furnish adequate moisture for the seeds. But check the box daily to be sure the medium is damp, never wet. And make sure it is never dry. When the seeds start to germinate, uncover the case for a few hours each day; in a few more days move the case to a bright window. When the seedlings have a few leaves, lift them from the growing medium with a nail file. Then prepare small holes in moist fine soil in shallow pots with ample drainage facilities and place one seedling in each hole, several seedlings to a container. Firm the soil around the young roots and continue to let the plants grow where it is bright and warm. When the seedlings are large enough—so that leaves touch—transplant them to individual pots. They are then ready for regular feeding with a very weak fertilizer.

One tried and tested method of germinating seeds is in gallon pickle jars. Wash and clean the jar, put it on its side, and prepare a 1-inch layer of damp propagating mix at the bottom. Sow the seeds, pressing them into the mix, and screw the top on the jar. Leave the jar on its side and place it in a warm spot. Water collects and runs down the sides of the glass to furnish moisture for the seedlings. After they form a few leaves, remove the top of the jar for a few hours each day. In a few more days the young plants are ready for the next move.

STEM CUTTINGS

I keep a jar of water containing some charcoal chunks at a kitchen windowsill where it is warm, bright, and somewhat humid. I fill the jar with cuttings of Angel Wing and Semperflorens begonias. In a few weeks, sometimes less, the cuttings have roots, and I plunge them into 3-inch pots filled with rich loam. As a result, I have more begonias than I know what to do with. Growing new plants from stem cuttings is an easy and generally successful method of propagating most upright and branching begonias. My jar-of-water method may be unorthodox, but it is fun.

I am often asked what is the best medium in which to root cuttings. I have at times used vermiculite successfully. Sand, perlite, and other media are also successful. The best advice I can give is to try them all and select the one that does best for you.

Because some begonia cuttings are delicate and need protection from dry air and drafts, place them in a propagating box. Take cuttings from a healthy stem in early spring when the parent plant is making new growth. Be sure the cutting has two nodes (swollen joints on stem). Remove the leaves and dip the stem into root hormone powder. Then insert the cutting upright in the starting mix so that the junction of leaf and stem rests in the mix, because this is where the new plant starts. Provide adequate humidity, about 50 percent, and when the roots are a few inches long, pot the cutting.

Leaf Cuttings

There are many ways to get new begonias from leaf cuttings: leaves, leaf and stem, leaf wedges, heel cuttings, leaf cones. Whatever method you select, be sure the cuttings have adequate moisture. I take a mature leaf with a short piece of stem and sink it into the rooting medium in the propagating box—but I am not always successful.

Rex begonias are usually propagated from leaf cuttings. Cut the leaf in wedges at the junction of the blades. (Use a sterile razor blade). Then place the leaf in the mix, making sure there is contact between the leaf and the growing medium. Weigh the leaf down with a few stones. Roots develop at each cut, the new plants drawing nourishment from the mother leaf. Leaf cones are leaves with the center portion cut within the apex of each of the main veins, creating a circular strip. Wrap the strip into a loose cone and place it cut edge down in the rooting medium. Fill the void of the cone with more mix, to about half an inch under the surface. Place in a warm, humid spot away from drafts, and keep the leaf cone moist, not wet.

Rhizome Cuttings

Rhizomatous plants produce plants quickly from rhizome cuttings. Take tip cuttings from the pointed end of the rhizome with a growing eye (node) on top and one on the bottom. Remove larger leaves, and dust cuts with powdered charcoal. Insert the rhizome either upright or horizontal in the mix in the propagating case. If you want several plants from the same rhizome, take larger pieces and cut them into 2-inch sections. Treat them the same as tip cuttings. In damp weather, rhizomes may rot. Take the necessary precautions and disinfect them with sulfur. With rhizome cuttings keep the planting mix just moist, never wet. When roots form, put the plantlets in a light soil. Continue to water them with care. When the leaves form, the plants can be given regular watering.

Heel Cuttings

If you are having trouble propagating a specific begonia by stem cuttings, try the more dependable way: take heel cuttings. Cut a leaf with a heel or swelling at the end of a stem. Cut well behind the bud growth in the axil. Dust the cut with sulfur, and anchor the heel cutting in the rooting mix with wire. Keep it warm and moist.

How to Hybridize Begonias

Hybridizing begonias is fascinating fun for all growers—professional or amateur. It is full of surprises, sometimes frustrations, but always satisfying when you see your own plants. The begonia growth cycle is rapid, which makes it easy for a novice to discover a new begonia or to raise one of his own crosses without endless waiting. A new and different begonia is indeed an achievement.

You can hybridize begonias for the fun of it or work from a planned program, with a definite goal in mind. Perhaps you want Rex plants with more abundant large flowers. That would be an accomplishment—or—a blue begonia. The possibilities are limitless. We are a world of dreamers. Some of those dreams have come true in the large tuberous begonias that have gained worldwide recognition.

For a beginner, it is easier to mate plants from the same

group; the chances of fertile seeds are better. The dominant characteristics of the parents are important factors for you to know. From past experience of hybridizers we know that *B. boweri* hybrids pass on the stitched leaf. *B. kenworthyi* offspring usually have purplish foliage; and Semperflorens—strong parents—crossed with other types almost always produce Semperflorens.

Some begonias make better parent-candidates because they are more likely to be fertile or to set seed. *B. boweri, dichroa, fuchsiodes, imperialis, manicata, metallica* are well-known robust parents.

Begonias produce separate male and female flowers. The male blossom usually blooms first and is larger than the female flower. It has reflexed petals when the pollen is ripe. The female has a winged ovary below the petals. In the center is the yellow pistil consisting of the ovary and stigma. When the female blossom is open and receptive (when the end of the stigma is sticky), remove the male blossom from the plant and, holding it by the petals, dust the pollen over the pistils of the female blossom. If the pollen is ripe and the pistil receptive, seed will set. Since timing is important—the pollen must be ready, the female flower fully open—it is sometimes necessary to store the pollen a short time. Pick the male bloom and put it in an airtight container in your refrigerator. To test for ripe pollen, lightly touch the stamens of the male bloom; a tiny amount of pollen comes loose if it is ready.

You can also use a soft paintbrush to transfer the male pollen to the female pistils. Label the fertilized flower, and keep records to avoid confusion.

Disappointments occur frequently in hybridization. It is quite possible that a pollinated flower may drop without setting seed or that a ripened pod is not viable. In that case, try again. Sometimes it takes a little practice. When the seeds have ripened in the pod, they are brown and dry. Then they can be planted. Whether you hybridize for fun or purpose, keep complete records on both parents and the results. If when the seedling starts to grow you think you have a truly different and unusual begonia, submit it to the American Begonia Society. They will grow it for you and observe it and officially register the name. And the naming of the plant is your preference.

5 BEGONIAS INDOORS

Growing plants under controlled light is a wonderful way of gardening and has made it possible for many to keep plants in otherwise useless space.

Though I have grown many different plants under artificial light, begonias and gesnerias have been the most satisfactory. I have two 49-inch trays with movable canopies. I find that the Angel Wings, Rhizomatous, and Rex begonias flourish and have as fine flowers and foliage as they do in the plant room. The Rexes do best. I do not grow miniatures under lights because they get too big. Some begonias are dormant in winter; under artificial "sun" they are inclined to keep growing.

There are several kinds of fluorescent lamps: cool-white, daylight, warm-white, and natural white, and lamps specifically for plants such as the Gro-Lux tube by Sylvania and the Plant-Gro tube by Westinghouse, both available at most hardware stores. I use two 40-watt Gro-Lux and two standard 40-watt cool-white tubes 48 inches long for a commercial metal planter and tray with an adjustable canopy. I add a 2-inch metal liner to the tray (not absolutely necessary) to hold pebbles, and paint the inside of the canopy white to reflect more light. At one end I keep a hygrometer to measure humidity. At the other end a thermometer. I aim for 74 F. by day, 64 F. at night, with humidity at 40 percent. Remember, the nighttime drop in temperature is important for healthy plants.

Much advice is given to gardeners about proper distance between the top of a plant and the bottom of the tubes. I don't understand this concern. Some of my begonias are 3 to 4 inches from the lights, others 6 to 7 inches; some even touch the tubes. It doesn't seem to make any difference. More important to me is the spacing of plants. I avoid crowding and I am careful to provide bottom ventilation—a trick I learned from growing orchids. I use redwood slats spaced 1 inch apart over the trays. My lamps, controlled by an automatic timer, burn 15 hours a day, from eight in the morning until eleven at night.

The most beneficial light for the plants comes from the center of the lamps; plants at the ends do not grow so well. I replace the tubes about every nine months because brightness depreciates as the lamp ages. But I never replace all four tubes at once; intense brilliance can be a shock to some begonias.

Artificial light cannot miraculously create plant growth. All cultural factors must be considered and, as far as I am concerned, recorded. Otherwise, I lose track. From my index cards I know that begonias under lights require more water and more fresh air than plants at windows. They grow faster because conditions are almost ideal, and they need more ferilizer too. Unlike natural light, which can be radical, constant intense fluorescent light accelerates growth so that the nutrients in the soil are quickly consumed by the plants. I fertilize the fluorescent garden at every other watering.

PLANT ROOM

Areas set aside especially for plants—garden rooms, plant rooms, California rooms, Florida rooms, solariums—become more popular every day. Many greenhouse begonias can now be grown successfully in these places. A plant room, whether it is large or small, quickly becomes the center of attraction.

The area can be in any part of the house, but if possible,

its floor should be waterproof. My garden room has a brick floor—tile, slate, or marble can also be used. If the floor is subject to water stain, place metal drip pans (made at sheet-metal shops) against the moldings to catch excess water. You can add white pebbles to the liners to make them look attractive.

Glass shelves at windows are excellent for plants. Because 3 shelves accommodate about 25 begonias, only one window is needed for a colorful garden. You can buy packaged units of brackets and glass at hardware stores or you can use wood shelving instead of glass. Floor-to-ceiling suspension poles are another idea. Trays fasten to brackets that fit into the poles. Each pole holds 8 trays.

Any room, any space with windows can become a garden area where you can enjoy morning coffee amid pleasant greenery.

In Greenhouse

General home conditions suit most begonias, but some kinds do require more warmth and humidity. And since greenhouse conditions are controlled conditions, they are ideal for most begonias. Generally, greenhouse plants do not need to be watered as frequently as plants in the home; in a greenhouse there is more humidity—many plants growing together create additional moisture in the air—and so the soil stays moist longer. Adequate ventilation is vital; although begonias do not like drafts, a buoyant atmosphere is necessary for their good health. Even with good ventilation, additional movement of air is sometimes required to keep the plants healthy. A small electric fan works well.

Begonias in a greenhouse must be checked frequently for insects. A general all-purpose spray should be used on a regular schedule.

Most begonias cannot tolerate direct sunlight, so green-house glass should be whitewashed for the greater part of the year—from April to November, depending upon your specific location. Or use the convenient bamboo roller blinds now available for greenhouses.

When placing plants, put Rex begonias on the floor because they love dampness and shade. Rhizomatous kinds look best on waist-level benches, and the Angel Wings thrive on the upper shelves where there is space for the pendent bowers of flowers. And don't forget some hanging baskets of begonias for dramatic accent.

Gift Begonias

During the holiday season, and at other times too, begonias are given as gift plants. Keeping them in beauty for as long as possible and making them permanent residents of my indoor garden has become a challenge to me. I hate to see plants discarded when with a little care they can be kept growing.

Remember that the florist begonias were grown under ideal conditions. It is a shock to a plant to be transferred from greenhouse to home. It may wilt or lose a few leaves before it adjusts to new conditions.

Keep gift begonias cool, about 65 F., and water moderately. After peak flowering is over, prune the plant severely and repot it. Put it in a warmer area, about 72 F., where there is good light. Water it sparingly for the first few weeks; when growth is established, increase moisture.

Most gift begonias are the winter-flowering tuberous varieties of *B. heimalis* and *B. cheimantha*. The *Cheimantha*, sometimes called "Busy Lizzie," is now improved and has a better chance to succeed in the home. Bushy plants with clouds of flowers, the *Cheimanthas* bloom from December to May. The *Heimalis* group is more showy but more fussy. They want it cold, 50 F., and I have rarely been successful with them.

BONSAI AND TREE FORM

Begonias trained as bonsai plants are unique, attractive, and grow amazingly well in this manner. Of course, as with all bonsai plants, a great deal of patience is necessary. Then, too, in most cases the small begonias will not flower as they do in ordinary pots. Still the bonsai plants are charming, and it's certainly worth while to have a few in the growing area. The tiny leaves and gnarled growth of many miniatures make them perfect for this sculptured kind of growing. Select a suitable bonsai pot; there are hundreds available now. Put a sandy base at the bottom of the pot and use a rich loam for planting; perhaps a layer of live moss over the soil for an attractive finish. When planting bonsai begonias, press the soil in well so every corner of the container is uniformly firm. Soil must retain moisture.

Since most begonias do not have extensive roots, excessive trimming is not necessary. Merely put the drainage material in the bottom of the pot. Try the plant in the container before potting it to determine whether you want a horizontal or a vertical effect. Fill in and around with soil and water gently until all the soil is wet. Wait a few weeks until the plant is established before shaping it.

Water the plants only when they are dry. A saturated soil should be avoided. The plants do best in light rather than in direct sun. Generally, close observation is necessary to attain the desired effect with bonsai.

Because I want my bonsai begonias to stay small, I do not feed them.

Excellent for bonsai are *B. dregei* and *B. digswelliana* because they have natural gnarled growth and tiny leaves. To me, they vie for attention with any small cedar or Japanese pine. The somewhat larger *B. fuchsiodes* is also suitable, and the wonderful *B. foliosa*, with drooping shiny green leaves, is especially handsome as a bonsai. It certainly looks like a tiny tree. Many of the medium-size begonias, like 'Erythrophylla' and *B. strigillosa,* twist and twine naturally and can also be used for bonsai. Although growing begonias in this way may not be the true art of bonsai (where it takes many years to train a plant), it is fun and the plants do quite well.

By accident I discovered that begonias can be trained to tree form. My *B. vitifolia* had lost all its lower leaves but continued to grow; as new leaves branched they too died. When the plant was about 16 inches high, I moved it to a warmer place; top leaves sprouted, and in a few months I had a begonia tree. It was so handsome I tried for the same effect with *B. kellermanni* by keeping it cool, letting the leaves die off. It is now an attractive tree-form begonia.

Depending upon the begonia used—some are more prone to this type of growing than others—many tree-form begonias can be grown. By snipping off bottom leaves, the flower head can be started at any height. Stake the stem; use bamboo sticks.

Of course, begonias grown in this manner will not be so tall or so bushy as fuchsia or geranium trees. However, they are unusual enough to attract attention even if they are only 12 or 16 inches high. The woody-stemmed *B. venosa* can be grown to about 20 inches.

BEGONIAS IN TERRARIUMS

There are many small begonias (see under "Miniature Begonias," Chapter 7) for terrarium planting. They grow beautifully in diminutive housings. The humidity created in these landscapes makes the plants flourish.

Terrarium planting in a crystal container or snifter or aquarium requires some work. It must be well planned, perhaps sketched on paper. Shape the contour of the soil, about 1 inch, to form the floor. Remove each begonia from its pot, spread the roots on the floor of the aquarium, and fill in and around with soil. After planting, mist the soil and foliage. Do not water too much. Keep the soil rather dry because excessive moisture rots the plants. Cover the terrarium with a piece of glass. Remove it for a few hours a day or in the evening to allow air to circulate through the dwarf garden. A north or west window is the best location for the terrarium.

6 *BEGONIAS OUTDOORS*

In May, many of your begonias can go outside. Natural air currents and rainwater refresh plants and make them grow lavishly. Use them as spot decoration for patios or porch or put them in window boxes for a row of color. If you have temperate climate all year, you can grow begonias in the ground as garden plants.

Where summers are short, it is best to leave them in their pots and put them outside for a summer vacation. Then it is easy to move them about, and there is no problem taking them in when cool weather starts. You can set a pair of potted begonias at your front door, decorate a fence with them, or have them in one concentrated area, perhaps under a tree. It is best if the pots are sunk to their rims in the soil. Dig out the soil and fill the hole with some small cinders to discourage insects from entering the pots. Then set the pots in the ground and fill in and around with fresh soil.

In summer potted begonias can decorate outside porches —Angel Wings, fibrous, and some Rhizomatous types. A few Rex begonias can be placed in the garden in a shady, moist area under a tree.

Outdoors, exposed to natural air currents and hot dry weather, begonias need daily watering. Misting the growing area will help to create the necessary humidity. Because strong winds can ruin begonias, place plants in a protected place. Direct midday sun is to be avoided, but most begonias need some early-morning or late-afternoon sunshine.

A lath house is always good for growing begonias. A canopy of 1- by 2-inch redwood spaced 1 inch apart will break the sun's rays and provide ideal light for most plants. It affords cooler temperatures too, and the enclosed area also helps to create additional humidity. Lath-house growing is easy, and all kinds of begonias flourish in one.

I grow many begonias on an outside deck. In January, February, and sometimes into March, when the temperature goes below 50 F., they must have protection from the weather. I use a heavy plastic sheet over a lath structure.

In the fall, usually after Labor Day (again, unless you live in temperate year-round climate), you must take your begonias indoors. Although several kinds will tolerate 45 F., I feel it best to provide them with extra warmth. Before returning the plants to the house, spray them with a general all-purpose insecticide and inspect pots and soil to be sure you are not carrying insects indoors.

Watering depends on rainfall, but generally the plants should be moist at all times. In temperate regions, Angel Wing and cane begonias planted in the garden become large bushes, certainly desirable. Unfortunately, in most parts of the country we must be content with smaller, less robust versions in pots.

Begonias in the Landscape

Begonias in the landscape are unusual and attractive. If you have an area that has large trees or a natural elevation, you might reserve it for a begonia garden. First lay out the location on a piece of paper—like a blueprint—so the plants complement the natural setting. Try to determine the mature size of the plant when you buy it, to avoid a cluttered look later. As I said before, if your season is short, grow begonias in pots plunged into the soil and camouflage the tops with rocks or stones or sphagnum moss. If you are planting directly into the ground, you will need raised beds and prepared soil. In either case make sure the drainage is perfect.

Rhizomatous begonias are best as foreground planting or as borders. Cane begonias should be used only as background, because they can become overpowering. Angel Wings are stunning with cascades of flowers, and will often bloom all summer. Do not crowd too many of them in one place; they grow rapidly. Choose plants with regard to their sun and shade requirements.

Here are some begonias that I have grown successfully in the garden:

B. acontifolia bears abundant white flowers. The scalloped dark green leaves are splashed with silver. Excellent for background planting. A good tall grower that needs bright light, no sun.

B. barkeri has bright green leaves with red edges and showy pink blossoms. Grows to a large size. Needs some sun and moderate watering.

B. convolvulacea is a climber. It has lovely light-green oval leaves and pretty white flowers. Likes to be grown somewhat moist and cool.

'Joe Hayden' is a rampant grower with large star-shaped almost black leaves. A dramatic plant. Keep it somewhat dry and in shade.

'Maphil,' often called 'Cleopatra,' is popular because of its chartreuse foliage and pink flowers. Tolerates morning sun.

B. nelumbifolia, the water-lily begonia, has lotus-like leaves and white flowers. Charming and amenable to adverse conditions.

B. popenoei has large pointed green leaves, slightly hairy. Lovely white flowers. Needs bright light, no sun.

B. scandens is an attractive climber with small pale-green leaves.

'Skeezar' has green and silver leaves, and needs full light.

Tuberous begonias for the garden are discussed at the end of this chapter.

CLIMATE AND BEGONIAS

Some climates are ideal for Angel Wings—growing them can be almost too easy. In other locations they refuse to respond no matter how much attention they are given. Tuberous begonias grow with little effort in California; in other areas they are a constant challenge. We cannot control weather, but we can select the begonias that do best in our locales. Here are some suggestions I have gathered while talking with begonia enthusiasts in various parts of the country.

In Florida, from Orlando south, cane-stemmed, Rhizomatous, Angel Wings, and Semperflorens are grown successfully outdoors all year. Protection is occasionally needed during a storm. Plastic sheets or tarpaulins do the job. The most successful collections I saw were under lath structures. Tuberous and Rex begonias are rarely grown in these warmer areas.

In the Midwest I have seen tuberous begonias and wax begonias grown in protected areas. However, most people keep them potted, because the season is short, from June to Labor Day. In extreme heat in August, tuberous begonias must be misted daily. A few Rex plants are grown, and I noticed many lush specimens of hairy-leaved begonias on porches and patios.

Cool nights usually prevail in New England, and tuberous begonias thrive there. Other begonias, like Angel Wings and Rhizomatous, are grown in pots to furnish patio and porch decoration during the summer months. Calla-lily begonias do extremely well here, better than in most areas.

In Seattle, cool nights and intermittent rain produce the largest tuberous begonias I have ever seen. They are absolutely stunning. Some cane-type begonias grow outside despite the cold, but I think these are exceptions.

In Minnesota and Wisconsin, potted begonias of many types are grown, and exceptionally fine Rex begonias are often seen on porches in summer. Calla-lily types do well too.

Tuberous begonias thrive around San Francisco; other kinds—and many are grown in this area—need winter protection. South of San Francisco, Santa Barbara is a natural growing ground for hundreds of begonias. And in San Diego I have seen what I consider the finest specimens of Angel Wing and other branching begonias growing in gardens.

OUTDOORS IN CONTAINERS

The choice of indoor containers is, as we have seen, adequate, but the selection of outdoor containers is limitless. Begonias with their diversified leaf coloring and shallow roots are ideal plants for container gardening—outdoors as well as in. They have long been used in window boxes. Now grown in decorative tubs and urns on patio or terrace, they again prove their versatility.

The mahogany-leaved Semperflorens begonias in small terra cotta pots grouped around a post or in the corner of a patio are cheerful and pretty. In large round stone containers, Rhizomatous begonias with large hairy leaves are showpieces. A small shallow bowl at the end of a terrace wall offers a rush of color in summer when filled with trailing begonias 'Alpha Gere' and 'Limminghei.' I cannot think of finer hanging plants. In baskets, too, or in redwood boxes they give a harvest of bloom for little care.

Soy tubs, kegs, or barrels of tall Angel Wings are effective for patio, terrace, and atrium. They grow quickly and easily. Perhaps you have a special begonia you want to show off. Put it in a Japanese porcelain urn, and it will immediately command attention.

When growing begonias outdoors, be sure they are not exposed to direct noon sun. This is not always easy in large open areas; it takes some planning and choosing. Late-afternoon sun is fine for most begonias; they grow lavishly. Begonias in containers need frequent and ample moisture. I water my outdoor plants every day from April to September. Where you live and how much rainfall you get determines your watering schedule.

Begonias in window boxes are superlative decoration; besides, they are easy to grow, and do not need a southern or eastern exposure. A bin of tuberous begonias is attractive whether viewed from inside the house or from outside.

Making a window box is easy. Redwood boxes are particularly attractive. I use 1 by 12 rough stock. The width of the window determines the length of the box. Usually, 3-foot length is good. Larger boxes are too hard to handle and when filled with soil weigh too much to be safely supported. My boxes are 12 inches deep, 8 inches wide. I use brass screws to fasten the sides together and I bore ½-inch holes 6 inches apart in the bottom so that excess water drains off readily.

To fasten a window box to the house, use sturdy metal brackets and attach them with lag screws to the house studs. If necessary use iron brackets for additional support. The box must be well supported at ends and center. Window boxes filled with soil weigh approximately 75 pounds per running foot, so a 4-foot box would weigh 300 pounds. With a very long box (over 36 inches), in addition to iron brackets I put chains on each end, which are secured by eye hooks at the rim of the box to the wall of the house.

Paint the iron brackets with a preservative so rust does not form. Otherwise, water running over them on to the house walls may stain the building.

Do not paint the inside of the box with a preservative. Begonias—as a matter of fact all plants—object to creosote or other wood preservatives. If you use redwood or cypress, no liner is needed; other woods require a metal liner or a polyethylene plastic sheet.

Natural redwood finish blends well with most house colors, but if you prefer, paint the outside of the box to match your home.

To look their best, window boxes need routine care. Faded flowers and leaves should be pinched off. In winter in most parts of the country, soil and plants must be removed from the boxes. Then cover the box with a plastic sheet as protection against winter weather.

TUBEROUS BEGONIAS

Begonias with tuberous roots have gained worldwide recognition, and rightly so. They are superlative plants. In full bloom they are wonderful to behold, for they offer a wealth of color. Some growers have been successful growing them indoors, but because of their rigid requirements for warm days, cool nights, and a good circulation of air, they are basically outdoor plants. Today's tuberous begonias, properly called Tuberhybrida, are intercrossed hybrids bred to near perfection in flower form, size, and color. They bloom profusely in all colors except blue. Whether in single pots or grouped together, they immediately add glamour to a patio, porch, or garden. In any location they are worth extra attention because they surpass any summer-flowering plant I know.

Most growers recommend copious watering for tuberous begonias. However, I find that drying out the soil somewhat between waterings is the best method for me. I have lost too many plants with daily watering.

HOW TO GROW THEM

In March, select large or middle-sized tubers—those an inch or more in diameter—from reputable dealers. Put a 2-inch layer of peat moss and sand (1-to-2 ratio) in a wooden flat or other suitable box. Set the tubers in the medium 2 inches apart and about ½ inch deep with the dented side up. Cover them with about ¼ inch of the mix. Roots develop from bottom, sides, and top, so be sure the tuber is covered. Place the flat in good light in 60 to 70 F. and keep the rooting medium barely wet. Too much water causes the tubers to rot. When the sprouts are about 2 inches tall (in about 2 weeks), shift them to shallow pots. I use a 4-inch azalea pot with a layer of stone and loose soil (2 parts loam to 1 part leaf mold). Move the potted begonias to a cooler place. Water them sparingly and watch for mildew or mealybugs.

In a few weeks, around the middle of May, the begonias will be ready for larger but shallow pots. Put them outside for summer bloom. Or put them in the ground if you want them for bedding plants. If plants develop too fast and become too large before danger of frost has passed, they can be held back by cool temperatures. Or if they are not growing fast enough, warmth will accelerate growth.

Like the orchids from countries of high altitude, tuberous begonias need good air circulation. They do best in pots in wall brackets on fences or in hanging containers where air circulates around the basket. There is a standard metal pot clip (available at nurseries) that attaches to brick or wood walls. It has a metal device that holds the rim of the pot. These are unique hangers, neat and simple, and take only a few minutes to install. Bracket and pot units are good too. The bracket attaches to the wall, and the arm or pot holder swivels so a plant can be placed at any desired angle. Wire baskets suspended from porch rafters or latticework are excellent because they allow air to circulate freely through the growing medium. Line the baskets with sheet moss. Wooden tubs and boxes are other suitable containers. They hold moisture, look well, and last a lifetime.

Place your plants where there is some scattered sunshine. Tuberous begonias survive heat during the day but must have cool nights, 55 to 60 F. If summer days are very hot, mist the area around the plants (*not* the leaves). Water begonias heavily on bright days, not so much in cloudy weather. When they are growing well, start using a fertilizer mixed half-strength every second week.

After flowering, when leaves turn dry and yellow, begonias should be watered sparingly. Let growth continue for as long as possible. Then take the pots inside. Lift the tubers and wash and dry them thoroughly. Store them in shallow boxes—I put them in metal baking dishes—at 45 to 50 F. Give them good air circulation but no light. Keep them dry until next spring.

Tuberous Begonia Flower Forms

There are a number of flower forms:

Camelliaeflora, most often seen, has a flat flower with incredibly large blooms in all typical colors. The ruffled form is fluted and frilled at the edges. There are endless varieties.

Cristata flowers are big, single, with a tufted crest on each petal, often a different color from the petal itself.

Fimbriata has frayed petals resembling carnations. These are robust bloomers with large leaves and erect flowers.

Marginata flowers have two forms: *Crispa marginata,* frilled singles with the same color edges; and *Double marginata* with petals lined and edged with bands of contrasting colors.

Narcissiflora has the center of its flower shaped like a trumpet.

Picotee has petals lined with a color that bleeds into the dominant flower color. There are picotees in camellia and rose form too.

Rose form has a high center of petals inside, and outer petals flared back like a rose.

Ruffled Camellia, large flowers in a wide range of colors.

Double Picotee, a summer flowering tuberous begonia with handsome flowers.

Named varieties include:

'Black Knight'—spectacular deep crimson flowers.

'Bonanza'—ruffled golden apricot; blooms 7 to 9 inches across. Currently available only from Vetterle and Reinelt.

'Chinook'—rose form with flowers 6 to 8 inches across; pure salmon color. From Vetterle and Reinelt.

'Flambeau'—lovely double orange-scarlet flowers.

'Frances Powell'—a nice double pink flower.

'Gaucho'—mammoth ruffled flowers of a deep orange. From Vetterle and Reinelt.

'Mandarin'—double salmon-orange blooms.

'Rosado'—deeply frilled and ruffled pink blooms. From Vetterle and Reinelt.

'Royal Flush'—a brilliant scarlet form of exceptional beauty. Vetterle and Reinelt.

OTHER SUMMER-FLOWERING TUBEROUS BEGONIAS

The Multifloras are a smaller group, compact in growth, with many flowers, either single or semidouble. They are good as garden borders and as windowsill plants. Easier to grow than other tuberous kinds, the Multifloras tolerate more sun and less humidity.

Some named varieties you might want to try:

'Ami Jean Bard'—apricot. Available from Antonelli Bros.

'Copper Gold'—double gold.

'Flamboyante'—single scarlet.

'Helen Harms'—double yellow.

'Mme. Richard Galle'—salmon. Available from Antonelli Bros.

'Rambouillet'—semidouble red.

'Sweet Home'—double red.

'Tasso'—semidouble pink.

The splendid hanging type tuberous begonia available in shades of orange or yellow or pink. Outstanding.

Hanging basket begonias are sometimes listed as pendulas or occasionally as Lloydi types by suppliers. Under any name they are magnificent flowering plants that produce hundreds of cascading blossoms all summer. Because of their floral abundance and vibrant color, perhaps they are the most beautiful of all trailing plants. Give them some protection from the wind and sun; keep them moderately moist. Plant two or three medium-sized tubers to a container. Pinch out young shoots early in the season to promote growth.

Here are some varieties that are very satisfactory:

'Andy Lee'—brilliant red. From Antonelli Bros.
'Cherie'—rose form, salmon. Available from Vetterle & Reinelt.
'Darlene'—pink blossoms with white centers. One of the best. From Antonelli Bros.
'Leza'—medium-sized blush-pink flowers. From Antonelli Bros.
'Lou-Anne'—clear pink flowers; very fine. From Antonelli Bros.
'Pink Shower'—lovely clear pink flowers. From Vetterle & Reinelt.
'Wild Rose'—deep pink. Four to five inches across. From Vetterle & Reinelt.

The hanging basket picotee tuberous begonia originated by Antonelli Bros. is not to be missed. Some flowers are edged with color, others heavily bordered and still others have a mottled coloring. They come in pink and rose shades, and in red, apricot, and salmon shades. The tubers are smaller than the standard hanging basket kind.

TUBEROUS BEGONIA SPECIES

These are the species tuberous begonias—the wild ones—responsible for our wonderful modern summer-blooming flowers. Although they are rare in cultivation, you will find them listed in catalogs. Some of the species are reputed to be difficult to grow, but I have not found this true. Generally, these plants need shade and drying out between waterings:

B. boliviensis. Handsome orange flowers; actually quite an amenable plant.
B. clarkei. A branching plant with deep-red flowers.

B. froebeli. Lovely gray leaves and vivid red flowers. Likes to be grown cool.

B. fulgens. A very small plant that has attractive red flowers.

B. micranthera. Several kinds: *B. fimbriata* and *ventura;* apricot flowers.

B. pearcei. One of the old-fashioned favorites with yellow flowers and brown-shaded leaves.

B. picta. Decorative green leaves splashed with bronze and brighter green. Pink flowers.

B. veitchi. A desirable begonia with very large red flowers.

PROPAGATION OF TUBEROUS BEGONIAS

If you have a choice tuberous plant and want more of them, there are two ways to get them: by dividing the tuber or from stem cuttings.

When bulbs start to mature in spring and show sprouts—just as soon as the new shoots are clearly seen but still not growing—cut the tubers into as many pieces as there are eyes. Dust the tubers with powdered charcoal and let them dry off for a few days. Then pot them 1 inch deep in sand and put them in a semishady warm spot.

For stem cuttings, take a 3- or 4-inch cutting of new growth with a sharp knife. Dust the cut surfaces with powdered charcoal before potting. Cuttings taken in spring and summer will root in about a month in sand and peat moss if put in a bright warm place. When roots have developed, pot the seedlings.

IN GARDEN BEDS

Because tuberous begonias in full bloom create a sensation in the garden, they are always worth a try even if you have very hot summers. Select a place for the begonias that has bright light. Remember not to put them under trees where there is little or no sunshine; you will have tall spindly begonias with only a few flowers, if any. Grow them in masses by themselves for a concentration of color. Use a good garden loam with fishmeal and prepare raised beds, about 4 inches off the ground, so that water can run off easily. Perfect drainage is necessary. Be sure the soil has enough humus so that it is not heavy.

Watering begonias outdoors depends on rainfall. In general, they should be wet but not soggy. On bright days, mist the buds frequently. Dry air causes buds to fall off without opening. On very hot days you might try early-evening watering instead of morning sprinkling. The soil is warm from the heat of the day, and late-afternoon watering cools it. Cool nights are preferable but not always possible, so hope for the best.

Feed plants in active growth with fish emulsion about every other week until September. But do not overfertilize. Remember that tubers are storehouses of food. Firm leaf texture and dark green color indicate a healthy plant. Blue-green color and rolled leaves indicate overfeeding. Let plants grow as late into fall as possible to store energy in the tubers for next season. After the first light frost, remove the tubers, clean and dry them, and store at 50 F. for next year.

7 THREE HUNDRED BEAUTIFUL BEGONIAS FOR YOU

SEMPERFLORENS BEGONIAS

Semperflorens are called wax begonias or ever-blooming, as their name indicates. And they do have the wonderful habit of blooming almost all year. They offer superior color to brighten the indoors and are also widely used for garden borders. Plants bear waxy glossy green, dark green, or mahogany-colored leaves, more uniformly round than most begonias. They were favorites in Grandmother's day, and are still sure to please.

Easy to grow, wax begonias do not take up too much space. In summer, they are ideal for the garden, take considerable abuse, and still put on a show. Some have single flowers, other semidouble and double blooms in shades from white to fiery red. Whether for windowsill decoration or for outside, these perky plants are tough to beat.

Give them sunshine and small pots, and forget about temperature and frequent waterings. They like to be dry: too much water rots them quickly. Repot these colorful begonias only when absolutely necessary; they like their roots crowded. Feed them regularly, once a week (they take more feeding than most begonias). Pinch back young plants once or twice to make them compact bushy specimens, and after peak flowering has faded, chop them back severely. This is not pleasant to do, but it is necessary. It is the only way for new growth to prosper, the only way to ensure another harvest of glorious flowers.

Semperflorens begonias are readily available from local greenhouses and mail-order companies. They are inexpensive, and new varieties appear frequently. My most recent one—'Carlton's Delight'—has fiery red flowers.

For a real show, use groups of wax begonias in planters or hanging baskets. They are excellent, too, for garden borders and charming in window boxes.

Most of my Semperflorens are in the garden, but in the Midwest I grew the following plants with success on an enclosed porch:

'Aloha,' double salmon orange.

'Andy,' a delightful dwarf with cupped green leaves, edged red. Pink flowers. Grows with little care.

'Ballet,' a handsome double white with striking bronze leaves. A neat compact-growing begonia; extra strong and free flowering. It well earns its popularity.

'Bo-Peep,' dark-bronze leaves with pink double flowers.

'Cinderella' bears crested pink blossoms tipped red. A delightful begonia that is strong, easy to grow.

'Curly Locks' grows upright with stunning dark-bronze foliage. Flowers are bright yellow.

'Dainty Maid' has cupped green leaves, white blooms.

'Ernest K,' rose-red flowers.

'Firefly' is attractive with crested fiery red flowers and dark-mahogany foliage.

'Green Thimbleberry' sports crested pink blooms and light-green leaves.

'Jack Horner' is a strong variety with miniature pink camelia flowers.

'Lucy Locket,' a good double pink "semp."

'New Hampshire,' pink blooms, robust.

'Othello,' orange-scarlet flowers.

'Pink Wonder' has double flowers, compact growth.

'Pistachio,' a charming miniature, bears pink petals, the center green changing to yellow as the blossom matures.

'Saga,' dwarf, bright red.

'South Pacific,' bright red with orange.

'Swanson's Pink' is bright and perky, with light-green foliage and large double pink flowers.

'Vernon,' bronzy red foliage.

'Westport Beauty,' sometimes listed as 'Gustav Lind,' is one of the original doubles. It has green leaves, pink blooms.

'Winkie,' compact, with dark foliage, rose flowers.

HAIRY-LEAVED BEGONIAS

These big furry-leaved handsome begonias have been favorite house plants for more than seventy years—a strong recommendation. Hairy-leaved begonias make even a beginner look good. The plants adjust to average home conditions; there is infinite variety in leaf shape and texture; and many of the species boast large trusses of flowers that are truly outstanding.

Botanically termed Hirsutes, these begonias have leaves flecked with short or long hairs, sometimes evenly spaced, sometimes far apart, or so close together that the surface is a silvery sheen of undulating color.

All hairy-leaved begonias are not in this group. Some Rhizomatous varieties have hairy leaves too. But the bearded flower is a general characteristic of the Hirsutes. Flowers are plentiful and pretty, white or greenish white to rose pink. The furry leaves are reminiscent of the plush furniture and flocked wallpapers of another era.

In winter, if I remember to put these begonias at a south window I have a bountiful crop of spring flowers. Those forgotten at a north or west exposure give me a small harvest. I shade the plants from hot summer sun with a window screen.

Because too much water kills Hirsutes, allow them to dry

out between waterings. Keep moisture from accumulating on the leaves, as this can cause rot. Temperature is unimportant—the hair on the leaves affords protection from cold—and 30 percent humidity is adequate for most in the group.

Here are some of my most dependable plants:

'Alleryi,' an old-time favorite, has frosted green leaves accented with purple. The pale-pink flowers are stunning at the window. Pinch out when young for well-shaped plant.

'Alto Scharff,' rather large, has fuzzy green leaves, red underneath, and bears white and pink flowers edged red.

B. bradei is delicate looking with small slim hairy green foliage. Flowers pinkish-white. Keep soil on dry side.

B. fernando costae is a low-growing, almost stemless plant. Its fleshy cupped green leaves make it worth all the attention it requires. It needs more water and pampering than most begonias. The white flowers add to its charm.

B. hugelli from Brazil is tall and stately with bright green leaves, red underneath; white flowers. Likes warmth.

B. incana (*B. peltata*) is rare, lovely. It has fleshy green leaves and white flowers. Grow it in shade.

B. laeteviridea has dark-green foliage; stems and branches are wine-red; white flowers. Grow in shade; dry out between waterings.

'Loma Alta' with really red plush leaves should not be missed. Grows easily with little care and becomes a specimen plant in a short time.

B. luxurians, ornamental with gray-green palmlike leaves. Wants warmth, bright light. Pot in shallow pots.

B. metallica bears pretty pink flowers with red beards. The foliage is handsome—silver hairs over dark-green purple-veined leaves. Put it in the garden in summer for a real show.

'Neely Gaddis' has green leaves with glistening white hairs; white flowers.

B. luxurians

B. roxburghi has decorative heart-shaped green leaves, fragrant white flowers. Likes it cool, 56 F.

'Rufida' is big, bushy, with large green leaves; pink flowers with red whiskers.

B. scharffi (*B. haageana*) is a robust hairy plant with large olive-green leaves and bountiful clusters of pink and white blooms.

B. *venosa*

B. venosa, fibrous rooted and hairy, is outstanding. The green cupped leaves are wrapped in tiny white hairs, like velvet. The thick stem has brown tissue-paper-like covering. This one does not like sun and prefers a dry soil.

'Viaude' has cupped olive-green leaves and bearded white flowers. A compact plant, it grows well with little care.

'Viau-Scharff' bears large olive-green foliage and white florescence. Water carefully; prefers dryness.

'Wooly Bear' or *B. leptotricha*, is a dwarf with succulent stems and shiny green leaves covered with fuzzy brown frosting. It is in bloom with white flowers six months out of the year in my home.

'Viaude,' a bearded beauty that grows well with little care.

'Wooly Bear' (*B. lepto-tricha*) is a popular standby. A good begonia that is almost always in bloom.

'Zuensis' is a charmer with puckered green leaves, somewhat red, and hairy deep-pink flowers.

The Hirsute group is large; here are more you might want to try that I no longer grow—a matter of space, not preference:

'Chiala Rosea.' Erect, bushy, with waxy dark-green leaves and pink bearded blooms.

'Crednerii.' Olive-green hairy foliage. Handsome large pink bearded flowers.

'Cypraea.' A branching plant with mottled green leaves; pink florescence.

'Drosti.' Very hairy round dark-green leaves. Large red bearded flowers.

'Lady Clare.' White blooms and hairy dull-green leaves.

'Margaritae.' Bushy, with small olive-green foliage, purple veined. Nice bearded pink flowers.

'Mrs. Fred D. Scripps.' Satiny green foliage, red veined. A vigorous plant with abundant white flowers.

'Prunifolia.' Smoky green cupped leaves. Grows erect and bears lovely white florescence.

'Vedderi.' Small pink bearded flowers and hairy green leaves.

'Vesperia.' Hairy green leaves; white blooms.

Angel Wing and Other Fibrous Begonias

The fibrous begonias are a large group divided into two sections here: the Angel Wings and miscellaneous kinds. The Angel Wings are heavenly house plants; their shapes and colors and the bounty of their flowers will put your head in the clouds. The wing-shaped leaves—one lobe longer and higher than the other—may be smooth and shiny or crisp and scalloped. Leaf color ranges from apple green to greenish brown with dots and spots of silver or white. Some leaves are veined and laced with design; others, lacy edged. The bamboo-like stems are branching and erect, the flowers abundant and magnificent. Clusters—as many as thirty flowers to a stem—cascade from stem joints and tips, so floriferous that frequently the plant itself is hidden in color. And this grand pageant occurs sometimes twice a year. Flower color is glorious. There are different shades of pink and red, salmon and orange, and white and off-white.

In favored climates, many Angel Wing begonias are suitable for outdoors. Grow them in sun and give them an east or west exposure for abundant flowers. An average humidity, say 30 percent, is adequate. Do not keep the plants moist all the time; rather, soak them and allow them to dry out before watering again. Prune the larger ones to promote growth of side shoots. Otherwise, they have a tendency to be leggy. In my plant room the shelves of Angel Wings are almost always a rush of color.

Here are some I have found superior for flower production:

B. acutangularis has pointed ruffle-edged green leaves and pink flowers. Grows well for me; not at all fussy about temperature or watering.

B. albo-picta sports small green leaves with silver spots. Pendent white flowers.

'Alzasco' is erect with very dark-green leaves, silver spotted. The flowers are brilliant red. Another easy one.

'Argentea Guttata' is the well-known "trout leaf begonia." The creamy flowers are tinged with pink. Likes afternoon sun.

B. coccinea has lovely bright-green shiny leaves, red flowers. Also other types with pink blooms. Give plenty of water.

'Decorus' has green leaves and sparkling white blooms.

B. dichroa from Brazil is low growing with bright glossy green leaves. The vibrant orange flowers make it a "must" in the indoor garden. Likes sun and warmth.

'Di-Erna' blooms freely with lovely coral flowers when potbound. This one has great vigor. Outstanding.

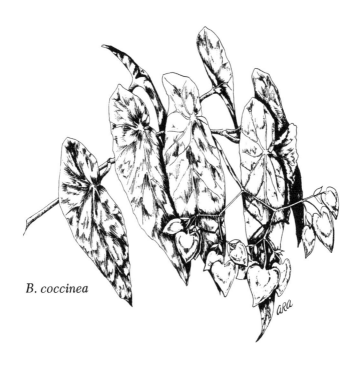

B. coccinea

'Grey Feather'

'Elvira Swisher' has large lobed leaves laced with silver; pink blooms.

'Grey Feather' is a great favorite with gardeners. It has slim arrow leaves, dark green, almost gray. The flowers are white with a pink hue. Grows like a weed; tends to get leggy.

'Gigi Fleetham,' a new variety, brings bronze foliage and white color to the windows.

'Interlaken' is robust, loves to grow, and quickly fills a pot with scalloped leaves. Decked in red flowers, it puts on a grand show in winter.

B. *maculata,* a popular begonia, has silver-splotched foliage and pink blooms. A difficult plant that needs high humidity.

'Pink Spot Lucerne' bears large red flowers; the green and pink foliage is handsome. Grows easily.

'Pinafore' is striking. It is low growing with slate-green leaves, beet red underneath. It bears pretty bright pink flowers and blooms readily with little care.

'Pink Rubra' has bright-green pointed leaves and large pink flowers. Likes sun, warmth.

'Pink Wave' with pink blooms and narrow green leaves makes a good basket plant. Sun, warmth.

'Silver Song' has silver-spotted leaves, bright-pink flowers.

'Spring Song' has small bright-green leaves, delicate pink flowers.

'Sylvan Grandeur' is bright with pink blooms. The foliage is heavily textured with pretty pink dots, red underneath. Grow somewhat dry.

Here are some more Angel Wing begonias that I no longer grow but that you might want to try:

'Constance.' Bronze-green leaves, pink flowers.

'Douglas Nesbit.' Drooping umbels of pink flowers; green leaves.

'Helen W. King.' Silver-spotted foliage, pink blooms.

'Laura Eglebert.' Pink flowers with dark-red foliage.

'Orange Parade.' Silver-spotted leaves; huge clusters of orange flowers.

'Pink Parade." Wavy silver-spotted leaves, salmon flowers.

'Robinson Peach.' Pink blooms; narrow green leaves dusted with silver.

'Romance.' Silver-splashed green leaves; large pink flowers.

'Rubaiyat.' Clusters of salmon flowers; smooth green foliage.

'Sara-Belle.' Green foliage with a pink hue; white and pink flowers.

'Shasta.' Fine white flowering coccinea hybrid.

'Velma's.' Red flowers and green cupped leaves.

Miscellaneous Fibrous Begonias

This is a catchall for begonias that do not belong to any one group because they have characteristics of two groups. I call it the outcast society, but in it there are some splendid members. Some are tall and branching; others have exquisite textured leaves. The variety is fascinating.

These begonias are for the adventurer because it is impossible to suggest cultural rules for such a diversified group. You are on your own, and if one method is not successful, you must try another. I have, though, a few clues for culture of some of these begonias and have mentioned them in the descriptions.

'Arabelle' is an Angel Wing type with metallic purple-green leaves covered with hairs. The blooms are pink.

'Brookes' is new from Logee's Greenhouses. A handsome plant with dark greenish-black leaves splashed with chartreuse veins.

B. cathayana is spectacular but temperamental. The plush leaves are almost purple, with silver and red veins; the flowers, vivid orange. A superior begonia that needs warmth and humidity, no drafts or direct sun.

'Orange Parade,' bowers of orange flowers. Grows like a weed.

'Brookes' is new from Logee's Greenhouses. Valued for its lovely foliage.

'Corbeille de Feu'

B. kellermanni

'Corbeille de Feu' is a fancy name for a fanciful begonia with red blooms and waxy green leaves. A good one, easy to grow.

'Digswelliana' branches freely, resembles a small tree. The shiny green holly-like leaves and bright red flowers make it handsome. Keep the soil reasonably wet at all times.

B. *kellermanni*, tall and ornamental, has deeply cupped green leaves covered with white felt; clusters of pink flowers in winter and spring.

B. *nitida* bears white flowers, shiny green foliage. Needs warmth.

'Oadi' has wavy green leaves and large pink flowers. Can take a little more sun than most begonias.

B. *parilis,* an upright branching plant with shiny green leaves and white flowers.

B. *roezlii,* erect and rangy, has smooth green leaves and pink flowers. Needs warmth, protection from drafts.

B. *sceptrum* (*aconitifolia*) bears silky dark-green leaves with depressed veins. Flowers are white, tinged pink. A tall, handsome begonia.

B. *schmidtiana* is a branching begonia with small hairy green leaves and pale pink flowers. A delightful one.

B. *serratipetala,* branching, pretty, has bronze-green foliage, pink flowers.

B. *tomentosa* is unique because it has succulent-like green leaves. The pink-rimmed white flowers are attractive.

B. *valdensium* is one of my favorites. The large grass-green leaves with etched veins surpass any foliage plant. Flowers insignificant.

Recent additions to my collection:

B. *alnifolia.* Pointed leaves tipped with clusters of white flowers. Keep on dry side.

B. parilis

B. sceptrum

B. schmidtiana, with delicate pink flowers and green leaves.

B. valdensium

'Arthur Mallet.' Exquisite red-bronze foliage and large pink blooms. Grow somewhat dry.

'Catalina.' Olive-green leaves, slightly hairy. Large pink flowers. Easy to grow, and lovely.

'Frieda Grant.' Pointed green leaves; pinkish-white flowers.

B. lubbersi. Unique. Dark-green leaves pointed at both ends, marked with silver, bronze, and red. Large white or pink pendent flowers.

'Marie B. Holly.' A sturdy good grower with waxy white blooms and glossy green maple leaves.

'Melisse.' Small silver leaves with black veins. Good foliage begonia.

B. lubbersi

'Catalina,' a fine variety with large pink flowers.

'Phyllomaniaca.' An erect grower with glossy green leaves and pink flowers. Spring blooming.

'Rosea-Gigantea.' A free-blooming begonia with red flowers, green shiny foliage.

'Ruth Anne.' "Crepe-paper" leaves that are green on top, red underneath. Lovely sprays of white flowers.

'Weltoniensis.' Large green leaves and pink flowers. Keep soil somewhat dry.

RHIZOMATOUS BEGONIAS

These are unusual begonias from Mexico and Central and South America. They are fascinating to grow—forever interesting. You never know what to expect, because there is such a large variety of them. Some are medium size and pretty, others are large and handsome. The leaves may be round or sharply star shaped; their patterns plain or fancy. Leaf texture may be satiny, smooth, or nubby, the foliage frilled or stained with brocaded colors.

The growth habit of the rhizome is an unusual added attraction. Some root as they skim the surface of the soil; others are compounds of plants; and still others run wild in flagrant branching. The rhizomes are food storehouses, so these begonias can endure—if necessary—a drought or freezing weather when underground. It is difficult to find better plants than Rhizomatous begonias. They tolerate neglect and still grow.

The tall-branched flower stalks with their clouds of bloom appear in early spring or late winter. Some plants have small cascading blooms, others, a pendulous florescence. In new types, the flowers are fewer but larger. A well-grown plant quickly becomes a lusty specimen suitable for home decoration. There are many time-tested old favorites: *B. masoniana* and 'Ricinifolia,' to name two. And new ones keep appearing all the time.

Grow these begonias in large shallow pots so the rhizome

can have ample room to grow on the surface. Root systems are not extensive, and deep pots of unused soil create sour conditions. Azalea or bulb pots are fine; they are shallow and always handsome. Water Rhizomatous plants with care. Too much moisture over too long a time causes the fleshy rhizomes to rot. Allow them to dry out thoroughly between waterings, and do not let soil get soggy. When in doubt about watering, mist the area around the plant. This gives the plant enough moisture to last until it gets a thorough watering the next day.

These begonias like to be pot bound—they grow better—so repot them only when absolutely necessary. Winter sunshine brings spring flowers, and a good growing temperature is 50 to 70 F. My plants thrive at 58 F. at night, ten degrees higher during the day.

In winter, some varieties take a short rest. Do not try to force them to grow. Water them sparingly, and try to forget about them until you see signs of new growth in early spring. Then water them regularly.

Most of my specimen plants are the old favorite Rhizomatous kinds. They have huge, stunning leaves, and make handsome pot plants for room corners. I grow many of them, but here are some I find the best:

B. acetosa is a special show from Brazil. It has hairy leaves on short stems. The top is silky green; underneath, it is vibrant red. A compact neat plant with lovely sprays of white flowers in spring. Needs warmth, bright light.

'Beatrice Haddrell' has small star-shaped leaves. They are almost black in color, with green veins. In spring, the top of the plant is crowned with pink blooms. Keep soil somewhat dry.

'Bessie Buxton' is adorned with pink flowers for more than six weeks. An upright grower, it has dark-green foliage. Takes abuse.

'Bunchi' is a splendid compact begonia with light-green or sometimes dark-green foliage, red underneath. The flowers are shell pink. A good one.

'Crestabruchi' is different and expensive and warrants its high price. The yellow-green leaves are heavily ruffled with twisted edges. After the pink flowers appear in late winter, water this one sparingly. It sometimes goes dormant.

B. decora has lovely white flowers and brownish-green leaves etched with chartreuse veins. A charming little plant. It needs warmth.

'Erythrophylla,' the "beefsteak" begonia also known as 'Feasti,' has round leaves, green on top, red underneath. Grows well in coolness and shade and bears pink flowers. A desirable begonia that withstands adverse conditions and still flourishes.

'Erythrophylla Helix' is a "sport" commonly called the corkscrew begonia because the round leaves are curled, and overlap the stems. Tall spikes of airy pink flowers crown the plant in early spring. Unusual; a good one.

'Fuscomaculata' has gray-green star-shaped leaves. Easy to grow.

B. goegoensis has dark-green round leaves with a reddish hue. Pink flowers. Give this one warmth and humidity.

'Bunchi,' sometimes called Lettuce Leaf begonia, is easy to grow.

'Erythrophylla' is easy to grow as a bonsai subject.

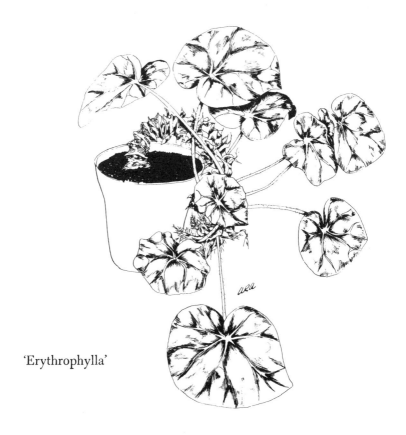

'Erythrophylla'

B. hemsleyana reminds me of a small palm tree. It hardly looks like a begonia because its green leaves grow in umbrella-like shape. Lovely pink flowers. Sensitive to temperature changes.

B. heracleifolia has green star-shaped leaves and pink blooms. An old favorite from Mexico, it has creeping rhizomes, hairy leaf stalks. Other varieties are: *B. nigrans,* with darker leaves and white flowers, and *B. sunderbruchii,* with dark green and bronze foliage. All varieties want warmth.

B. imperialis 'Otto Forster,' a stunning plant with heart-shaped dark-green leaves suffused with a green area, has white blooms. Low growing and compact. It needs shade and humidity.

B. manicata aureo-maculata is choice, one of the best of the *manicata* varieties. It has light-green foliage mottled yellow, and ruffled at the edges. It has a branching habit; one of my favorites.

'Maphil,' sometimes called 'Cleopatra,' appears frequently as a hanging basket plant, although it is not a trailer. But it does make a round compact ball of lovely color. The foliage is splashed with gold, chocolate brown, and chartreuse. In April, tall spikes dancing with tiny pink flowers make the plant a stunning sight. Flood, then allow to dry before watering again.

B. purpurea is a stunning plant with compounds of green leaves, red underneath, laced with red veins; frilly margins. Erect flower stem bears greenish-white blooms. Grows best for me on the dry side.

'Ricinifolia' might have graced your grandmother's living room. It resembles the castor bean plant and grows and blooms rapidly, usually in 18 months. The large leaves are green, flowers pink. Likes a sandy soil, summers outdoors.

'Skeezar' is a nice compact plant with green and white foliage.

B. heracleifolia

B. imperialis 'Otto Forster'

B. purpurea

'Maphil' is an old favorite. The attractive multicolored foliage looks good in basket or pot.

B. strigilosa has chocolate-brown spotted green leaves on long graceful stems. Flowers are blush white. Pinch off drooping leaves and stems; they are quickly replaced with fresh growth from the center of the plant. Keep plant in shade; sunlight scorches foliage.

B. vellozoana, with luxuriant foliage as nice as the fancy-leaved Anthuriums, is a must in a begonia collection. The iridescent leaves—chartreuse veined—glimmer and glow in bright light. Pure white, pink-haired flowers on tall spikes make this a sensational begonia. Grow warm.

Other desirable Rhizomatous begonias are:

'Alice.' Green pebbled leaves, flowers, greenish white.

'Carol Star.' Star-shaped bronze-green hairy leaves. Pale pink flowers.

B. chimborazo. A clumpy grower with leaves like the nasturtium. Pink blooms.

B. conchaefolia. A small plant with succulent green leaves; pink blooms. Likes warmth.

B. crispula. Shiny green round leaves and pink flowers.

'Congo.' Pointed olive-green foliage with light-green veins. Pink flowers. Outstanding.

B. dayi. Light-green foliage with red veins. Ivory flowers on long stems.

'Edith M.' Light-green leaves with chocolate-colored lacing. Hairy stem and pink flowers.

'Illustrata.' Handsome plant with a coat of fine white hairs. Pebbled texture. Pink flowers.

'Illsley.' Miniature and lovely. Dark-green foliage and pink blooms.

'Immense.' Mammoth star-shaped leaves. A mature specimen is outstanding. Pink florescence.

B. mazae. Round leaves that are bronze green. Light-pink flowers. I have never been successful with this plant. It requires warmth, humidity, and perfect drainage.

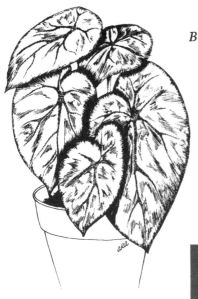

B. dayi

'Illustrata,' a handsome
begonia for windowsill.

'Ricky Minter.' Rose-pink flowers in winter. Dark-bronze
ruffle-edged leaves. Grows fast, but it is another one that
never has done too well for me.

'Sir Percy.' Pointed silver leaves with dark edges. White
flowers.

'Spaulding.' Bushy with decorative foliage; light to dark
green on top, beige underneath. Pink flowers.

B. squamosa. Creeping dwarf with glossy green, red-
trimmed leaves. Pink flowers.

'Speculata.' Marbled grape leaf, light green. Fine low-
growing plant with pendent white flowers. Decorative.

Left, 'Spaulding,' exquisite leaves on tall stems. Right, 'Speculata' is sometimes listed in catalogs as a Rex but is more often classified as Rhizomatous.

'Ricky Minter'

REX BEGONIAS

Coleus, crotons, and caladiums are attractive plants with multicolored foliage, but Rex begonias are even prettier, and well worth the effort that is required to grow them successfully. They are grown for their foliage, and the leaves —texture, color, and pattern—are unbelievably handsome. The Rexes with gold, silver, platinum, or bronze coloring are perhaps the most popular. But there are others in the group that are equally magnificent and match the painter's palette—red, green, garnet, blue, purple, black, brown, with wonderful texture. Some are like silk or satin, others like taffeta and velvet. Patterns run wild—splotched, blotched, or mottled, lined or geometrically designed, and some have colors fading into colors like a rainbow. All are stunning.

The original Rex begonia was discovered accidentally on an orchid plant at an auction in England in 1856. Since then hybridists have created and fashioned Rex begonias into the kings of foliage plants. There are miniatures as brilliant as precious gems, spiral types, and the *Diadema* kind with deeply cut leaves. Many are Rhizomatous plants with creeping runners that skim the surface of the soil, but there are also tall and branching ones. All bear pink or white flowers, and while some growers advocate snipping the blooms so the strength will be forced back to the foliage, I have grown Rexes both ways and can notice little difference in the plants. There are thousands of Rexes to choose from, and a well-grown specimen is always a conversation piece.

Rex begonias will be successful house plants for you if you remember that they love shade and humidity. Grow them at north windows and provide facilities for the extra moisture in the air. Most Rex plants take a nap in winter and lose some leaves. Do not discard them or try to force them to grow. In a few months, around the middle of March, they recover and are more beautiful than before.

The varieties with rough-textured leaves are somewhat easier to grow than the group with thin velvet-like foliage. However, none is impossible.

I use a loose soil with plenty of leaf mold and sand. Most of my plants are in small pots; I had trouble when I used large pots. The unused soil turned sour, and the plants perished. Keep Rex begonias moist but never soggy. If they dry out, do not be too concerned; soaking brings them back quickly. Keep plants out of drafts; they kill plants quickly. Provide a nighttime temperature of 62 to 67 F.

The species has become so mixed in the progeny that it is difficult to divide them into clean-cut groups. Many mail-order houses offer unnamed varieties, excellent for the beginner, and always a surprise, so do not hesitate to buy them. They are cheaper, too.

My Rex plants are grown with 60 percent humidity, 80 F. day, 68 F. night, in summer. The rest of the year they are grown at 76 F. day, 64 F. night.

Here are some of my favorites:

'Autumn Glow.' Rose colored, some silver.

'Black Diamond.' Dark maroon, center zone burnished silver.

'Burvel.' Green leaves with red hairs.

'Calico.' Small plant with crimson leaves mottled with silver.

'Can Can.' Lobed ruffled leaves, silver-gray with blush pink. Foliage has taffeta texture.

'Cardoza Gardens.' As alluring as its name. Large flamboyant foliage in all colors of purple, silver, and green. A really brilliant begonia.

'Curly Carnot.' Silver and green.

'Fantasy.' Shades of green.

'Fiesta.' Round leaves splashed with silver and pink. Very showy.

'Glory of St. Albans.' Metallic rose-purple foliage. Another popular showy begonia.

'Helen Teupel.' Silver and maroon.

'Huntington Lake.' Green foliage with silver spots.

'Kathleyana.' Large pointed leaves speckled with silver.

'Merry Christmas.' Striped with color, mostly red.

'Ojai.' Green, silver, and violet.

'Oregon Sunset.' Maroon, pink.

'Peace.' Metallic red, silver leaves.

'Queen of Hanover.' Light-green leaves banded with darker green.

'Salamander.' Strong grower with pointed silver and green foliage.

'Silver King.' Steel-gray leaves that glisten in light.

'Solid Silver.' Narrow foliage; silvery green.

'Stardust.' Large olive-green leaves dusted with silver.

'Thrush.' A unique upright branching plant with crimson red maple-shaped leaves dotted with silver.

'Winter Queen.' Spiral-form leaf, silver, purple, and pink.

And here is a list of some others according to their predominant leaf color. I hope this makes selection somewhat easier.

MOSTLY SILVER

'A. D. Davis.' Large leaves of silver-gray trimmed brown; a striking plant.

'Dark Carnot.' Silver-spotted foliage.

'Modesty.' Long leaves dotted and splashed with silver.

'Mrs. H. G. Moon.' Hairy leaves, silver, green, and pink.

'Peter Pan.' Dark-green leaves edged silver.

'Queen Wilhelmina.' Blistered leaves almost all silver; a mature plant is spectacular.

.   .   .

'Merry Christmas'

A fine group of specimen Rex plants.

MOSTLY GREEN

'Bearded.' Outstanding hairy Rex; all shades of green.
'Evergreen.' Broad tapering leaves of solid green.
'Orient.' Dark-green foliage.
'Silver Fleece.' Hairy green leaves stippled with silver.

MOSTLY PINK OR MAROON OR RED

'Aureola.' Pink suffused with silver.
'Crimson Glow.' Dark pink dusted with silver.
'Dusky Rose.' Maroon and black.
'King Edward IV.' Large red leaves with rose spots.
'Mountain Haze.' Deep rose dusted with silver.
'Pacific Sunset.' Different shades of red.
'Scarlet O'Hara.' Showy leaves, scarlet and red.

SPIRAL FORM

'Avila.' Rose, silver, and green foliage.
'Bronze King.' Bronze and green with pink hairs.
'Comtesse Louise Erdody.' Gray-green, flushed rose; pink hairs.
'Curly Merry Christmas.' Satiny red and bright green.
'Curly Silver Sweet.' All silver.
'Sunburst.' Gray-green; sunburst spot in center.

MINIATURE BEGONIAS

Small and pretty, colorful and easy to grow, these are winsome and wonderful, but dangerous. At times I become so fascinated with them I neglect my other plants.

Where space is a problem, it is difficult to find better plants than these charmers. They bear bright flowers, winter and spring, and some tiny varieties of the Rex group are veritable tapestries of color. Miniatures are at home in a terrarium or on a windowsill or in a dish garden. Most varieties grow slowly and need only minimum care to flower. In diminutive form—like bonsai—they compel attention. But watch out—these baby plants can steal your heart.

Use fine-textured soil to pot miniature begonias. Leave a fraction of space at the top of the pot to allow for watering. Small plants dry quickly, so check the soil frequently and keep it reasonably wet at all times, but never soggy. Feed miniatures carefully. Remember that you want them to grow slowly. Pinch and prune them to form pleasing shapes.

These mighty "mites" thrive in average home temperatures of 68 to 78 F. with 30 to 40 percent humidity. When placing the plants in the growing area, do not crowd them. Give each one space so air circulates around the leaves. Keep them in bright light, out of sun.

I grow dozens of miniatures. Here are some dependable ones:

B. aridicaulis is a delightful imp with tiny green leaves and white flowers. It never grows more than 6 inches high.

B. boweri, the "Eyelash Begonia," has green leaves stitched with black at the edges, and lovely pink flowers. There are several *boweri* varieties: *B. boweri major* has larger leaves. 'Bow Arriola' has green and purple foliage. 'Bow Chancee,' yellow and green leaves. 'Bow Joe,' small dark-green leaves, and 'Bow Nigra,' small star-shaped bronze foliage. *B. boweri marga-nigra* is new from Logee's Greenhouses, and surpasses the others. It has mahogany and green leaves clad in scant white hairs. Tiny white flowers make it perfect.

'Chance' is a chance seedling of a calla begonia with pink flowers and magnificent mottled leaves. Has tremendous recuperative powers. Mine was crushed when I took it from the shipping crate, but within a few weeks it came back with fresh growth.

'Chantilly Lace,' usually listed as a miniature, can grow

to 12 inches or more. Rhizomatous, it has cupped leaves, eyelash hairs at the edges. Pink flowers in winter.

'China Boy,' with notched bright green leaves and red stems, is a trailer. It bears lovely pink blooms. Because 'China Doll' is similar, you would probably not want both.

B. *dregei* is delightful, with small bronze-red "maple" leaves. Several kinds available, some larger than others.

B. *foliosa,* the fern-leaf begonia, is unusual. It looks like a tiny weeping-willow tree with arching branches and diminutive shiny dark-green leaves. The tips of the branches bear white flowers. Water this one heavily, and clip it if you want to keep it small.

B. *griffithi (annulata)* is appealing with heart-shaped downy leaves, ruby and emerald with rose bands and white flowers. Needs warmth and protection from drafts.

B. *hydroctylifolia,* the miniature pond-lily begonia, has glossy dime-size leaves. Pink flowers pop out in winter. Needs warmth.

'Louise Closson' has black leaves with irregular purple markings, pink flowers. Not easy to grow, but not impossible.

'Lulandi,' an Angel Wing, grows to 14 inches. It is a branching plant with bright-green leaves and large pink blooms.

'Orange Dainty' is a gem. The dark-green leaves are toothed at the edges, the orange flowers delightful. Grows easily for me in bright light.

'Red Berry,' a Rex, has wine-red foliage. A fine begonia that needs warmth and humidity.

'Red Wing,' also a Rex, has silver edges, wine-red leaves.

B. *rotundifolia* stays small for years with light-green round leaves and pink flowers.

'Rosa Kugel,' a wax begonia, has small green leaves.

'Star Bright,' a new miniature Rex, is lovely with silver dots on dark-green leaves.

'Chantilly Lace' is a decorative plant for coffee table or window.

Above, *B. dregei,* the maple leaf begonia, handsome for bonsai.
Below, *B. foliosa,* the popular fern leaf begonia.

'Lulandi,' a miniature that grows well under almost all conditions.

B. rotundifolia

'Winter Jewel' (*bartonea*) has frosty green leaves dusted with silver. Dainty white flowers in winter. Grow this one warm.

Here are some recent additions to my miniature collection:

'Albo Picta.' A cane begonia with narrow silver-spotted leaves and whitish-pink blooms.

'Baby Rainbow.' Delightful Rex with cupped silver green and purple foliage.

'Calico.' Somewhat large for a miniature. Rounded silver-dotted leaves flushed red.

'Ivy Ever.' Glossy green leaves, pink flowers. Good trailer.

'Medora.' A branching plant with small glossy green foliage and pink flowers.

'Ivy Ever,' one of the better miniatures. A charming plant.

'Pansy.' Dwarf Rex with pointed green leaves and metallic green overlay.

B. richardsiana. White flowers with green maple-like leaves.

'Virbob.' Star leaves, marbled green, chartreuse, bronze, and red. Pink blooms; a real delight.

BASKET BEGONIAS

Some years ago, before hanging baskets were available, I started making my own containers. Shelf and sill space in the plant room was crowded, but upper windows with bright light were empty. I decided to make simple wire baskets from inexpensive galvanized wire, found at hardware stores. I lined the baskets with sphagnum, and was ready to grow trailing plants.

Today, there is a wide selection of hanging containers, one prettier than the other. There are baskets of ceramic, redwood, clay, metal, and other materials in different shapes, sizes, and colors. Some are simple. Others, elaborate. Some have drainage holes, others do not. For begonias, a container that provides adequate drainage is necessary. Also good and still sold is the inexpensive wire basket (much the same as the ones I made). These have spaces between the wires to allow the plant roots to breathe, and drainage is near perfect.

Whatever container you use, unless you water plants at the sink, some kind of saucer or drip pan is needed to catch excess water. At one time I used 18-inch round metal birdbaths set on the floor. Recently, I have seen a plastic saucer that clips on the bottom of the open basket to catch water. These are now sold at nurseries.

Open-spaced wooden baskets or wire ones need to be lined to hold the potting mix. Sheet moss or sphagnum (unshredded) does the job quickly. Moisten the moss and place it firmly against the sides of the container. Place your plants by working from the center of the basket to the ends. The 8-inch-diameter basket about 5 inches deep is one I use frequently for trailing begonias.

Standard clay pots now come with drilled holes in the rim and wire hangers—these are fine containers for trailing begonias. They are often seen in California. One of my friends has created a striking effect by using three of these, more or less laced together. The top one hangs from the ceiling; the second one is attached with an eyehook to the bottom drainage hole of the first container, and the third pot is hooked in the same manner to the second. This gives a floor-to-ceiling column of green and a veritable fountain of colorful trailing begonias. The water dripping from one plant to the other does not harm the trailers.

Large shallow metal and fiber-glass circles are also used as baskets, attached with chains to the ceiling. But I find them too big; they have never been successful for me.

A group of begonias in a basket is always best. They look attractive. Do not put all plants on one side; place them in a circular pattern, allowing enough space between each one so they can grow. Or put them together in the center so they will grow out naturally. Be sure to grow varieties that require the same conditions. Specific hints are included with plant descriptions.

Use a light, porous, slightly acid soil for planting, and follow the same cultural steps as for growing other begonias. Do pinch out the plants occasionally to help promote branching. And some time after they have flowered, be sure to prune them to encourage fresh growth. Remember, it is necessary to cut back plants if you want new flowers. Almost any begonia grows well in baskets—the wax begonia, the flamboyant Angel Wings, the creeping Rhizomatous kind, and the magnificent summer-blooming tuberous Lloydi types.

A basket of begonias at eye level is dramatic and handsome. I have several in the plant room and in the house. This is superb decoration for little cost, and here are some of my favorites:

B. acuminata, a fountain of white flowers with contrasting soft-green leaves. This lovely plant grows well for me in warmth and humidity.

B. convolvulacea has glossy green nasturtium-type leaves. Bears white flowers in spring, and wants coolness, about 55 F.

'Corallina de Lucerna' is foolproof, showy. A large plant that grows rapidly, it bears bundles of red flowers. The cream-spotted green leaves add to its beauty. Grows almost under any condition, but must be severely pruned after blossoming.

'D'Artagnon,' popular and handsome, is sometimes called Queen of the Basket Begonias. It has forest-green foliage, grows rapidly, and makes a show. Give it lots of light.

'Ellen Dee' is a 'Limminghei' offspring with glossy green leaves and large clusters of orange flowers. Outstanding.

'Elsie M. Frey,' with pink flowers and metallic green red-lined leaves, is popular, easy to grow.

'Florence Carrell' has crinkly green leaves. The coral flowers make it a desirable begonia.

'Limminghei' blooms in late winter with lovely coral flowers. Shiny green leaves make this one a cascading beauty. A stellar hanging begonia. Likes warmth.

'Mme. Fanny Giron,' with large red flowers and green leaves, is for Christmas bloom. Grows well with little care.

'Orange Rubra' has clusters of orange flowers, pointed narrow light-green leaves. Takes more sun than most begonias, and puts on a show in midwinter for me.

'Pink Camellia,' a Semperflorens has dark-red leaves, pink flowers. A group of these makes a handsome basket.

'President Carnot' is popular because it blooms easily. The

'Elsie M. Frey,' splendid for baskets. Abundant pink flowers.

'Limminghei'

copper-green leaves are attractive, the flowers, pretty—usually pink, but can be red or carmine too.

'Shippy's Garland' has scalloped dark-green leaves, cascades of bright pink flowers.

Other basket begonias are:

'Alpha Gere.' Light-green toothed leaves. White flowers.
'Indra.' Small creeper with green leaves and white blooms.
'Lloydi Yellow.' English tuberous kind with lovely yellow flowers.
'Marjorie Daw.' Large bright-green leaves. Pink florescence.
'E. O. Orpet.' Bronze-green foliage. Red flowers in winter.
'Red Compta,' Shiny pointed red leaves and red flowers.

'President Carnot'

WINTER-FLOWERING TUBEROUS BEGONIAS

HEIMALIS

Introduced in London in 1883, these are big bold, colorful begonias crowded with flowers at bloom time. They are offsprings of the species *B. socotrana* crossed with high-altitude Andean tuberous begonias. The showy single or double flowers in shades of pink, salmon, apricot, red, or white are stunning. But such beauty is not easily harvested. The group is difficult to cultivate, exacting in its requirements. True to their heritage, these begonias need cool air—50 to 58 F.—and a buoyant rain-forest atmosphere, difficult to duplicate in the home. Small pots and coarse soil are other needs. My plants never did well in the Midwest, but in California, on an outside deck all year, they fare better. To save the plant for next year, after it has flowered, place it in a cool spot and water it sparingly until early spring. Then shake off the soil around the tuber, and repot it. Grow it cool, 64 F., and moderately wet through the summer. Keep water from the leaves. The *Hiemalis* group is often referred to as Clibran begonias, the Holland firm that originated one of the finest strains.

'Altrincham Pink' is to me the handsomest in the group. The flowers are double pink, and last a long time.

'Baardse Wonder' is new, lovely. It has deep-red flowers, black stamens. 'Baardse Glory' has pink flowers.

'Emily Clibran' is reputed to be the best in the group. It has double pink flowers.

'Exquisite' bears large single pink flowers.

'Fairy' has double pink flowers.

'John C. Mensing' is free flowering, low growing. The flowers are orange.

'Emily Clibran'

'Marietta,' large double apricot blooms.
'Nellie Visset,' double red rosebud type.
'Pink Perfection,' double pink.
'Rosalind,' single pink.
'Rose Queen,' a strong grower with lovely rose-colored flowers.
'Snowdrop,' a double white.
'Vander Meer's Glorie,' large orange flowers.

CHEIMANTHAS

This is the other offspring of *B. socotrana,* crossed with the African species *B. dregei.* Often sold as gift plants during Christmas, these make good houseplants but need extra attention. Grow them somewhat cool (70 F. day; 60 F. night). Keep them in a humid place with good ventilation. The soil must be moderately wet at all times but never soggy. Give them plenty of light but not much sun.

These bushy plants are loaded with bloom from December until May. Flowers are white or pink or sometimes almost red. After its flowering, cut back the plant severely. Keep it moist and cool. When the new shoots come from the base, cut them off and root them in a propagating case.

'Carolina' bears rose-pink flowers.
'Marina' is deep rose.
'Gloire de Sceaux,' beautiful rose-colored flowers.
'Lady Mac,' pink or white.
'Marjorie Gibbs,' a robust plant with pale pink flowers.
'Spirit of Norway,' vibrant red.
'Tove,' rose-colored blooms.

CALLA-LILY BEGONIAS

A form of Semperflorens, these begonias are covered with small white curly leaves at the tips of the shoots, and so their name, Calla lily. They have flowers in shades of pink or red (some double). Lovely and desirable though they are, they are also somewhat difficult. They need sun and coolness. Fresh air keeps the plants healthy, but drafts kill them quickly. Overwatering causes rot, but excessive dryness makes the leaves curl and die. Humidity helps to keep the plants healthy, but too much moisture in the air brings mildew. Theirs are difficult requirements to duplicate in the home, especially during the hot summer months, but I have been successful with some of the newer varieties— 'Cherry Sundae' and the 'Calla Queen,' which seem less touchy about culture.

My Calla begonias stay in 5-inch pots in a west window of an unheated porch. I keep them dry and cool, and I try not to pamper them too much. Kindness kills them. They must be cut back severely after flowering.

When taking shoots for new plants, include plenty of green leaves. A propagating box is necessary for these cuttings. Another way to get new Callas from old ones is by division. Take a small section of the crown of the parent plant and place it in a 3-inch pot with a rich soil. When roots fill the pot, shift the plant to a larger container.

'Calla Queen' is a strong grower with large green leaves and single pink flowers. One of the best.

'Charm' has yellow and green foliage with pink blooms. A dwarf plant, it is striking and desirable in the indoor garden.

'Cherry Sundae,' the double-red Calla lily, is a profuse bloomer. The red flowers are large, the white leaves handsome. Grows well at a bright window.

'Ruby Jewel' bears semidouble red flowers. Another strong grower, and certainly worth a try.

8 BEGONIAS FOR SHOW

Growing begonias soon becomes an addiction. After you grow a few of them, you will want to share your experience with other people interested in these fine plants. The begonia world is large. There is the American Begonia Society, with branch affiliations throughout the country, yearly shows, and conventions.

SOCIETIES, SHOWS, AND MAGAZINES

The American Begonia Society is a nonprofit organization affiliated with the American Horticultural Society, the American Horticultural Council, and the Los Angeles State and County Arboretum. The society offers invaluable aid in identifying begonias, making seeds available, and maintains a splendid research department. An annual membership fee is $2.50, and this brings you the monthly *Bulletin*, a magazine devoted to begonia growing. New memberships should be sent to Membership Secretary, 1510 Kimberley Avenue, Anaheim, California.

There are branch societies affiliated with the American Begonia Society in many cities. If there is one in your area, do join it. Meetings are usually on a monthly basis. It is a good way to exchange plants, gain information, and meet people who have the same interests you have.

There are also yearly shows held at different times throughout the country. This is where you can meet people from other areas to get different views about growing begonias.

National magazines often run begonia articles. Keep clippings; known authors on the subject offer invaluable information.

Exhibiting Begonias

Even if you don't think your plants will take first prize, enter them at shows. Many times I have seen hobbyists pleasantly surprised by winning a trophy or ribbon. If you are really out for awards, it is a good idea to specialize in one or two groups of begonias. Perhaps Rhizomatous kinds, or how about miniatures?

A printed program of schedules of classes of begonias is usually available before a show. Study this, and decide where your plants have the best chance of winning an award. These are the classes usually found in a show:

Fibrous Begonias

Tall types (over 3 feet)
Intermediate (18 to 36 inches)
Low growers (under 18 inches)

Hairy Begonias

Sparsely hairy
Heavily hairy
Distinct foliage

Rex Begonias

Miniature leaf
Small leaf
Medium leaf
Large leaf

Medium spiral leaf
Large spiral leaf
Branching type

Rhizomatous Begonias

Small leaf
Medium leaf
Large star leaf
Spiral or crested leaf
Unusual foliage
Hairy types
Rhizomatous (upright)

There are also awards for best-species plant, hanging begonia, begonia on totem pole, in planters and terrariums, in miniature gardens, and so on.

The begonias selected for showing should be well-groomed and well-grown plants. They should be at their best for show time. If your plant is not growing fast enough, give it more light and warmth. If it is growing too fast, move it to a cooler place.

Be sure that the outside of the container is clean and that the pot is in proper proportion to the size of the plant. Some tall begonias must be staked. Make the staking as nearly invisible as possible. All dead wood and faded flowers should be removed from the plant. Wipe foliage with a soft dry cloth. Don't use sprays. For delicate hairy-leaved kinds, use a discarded toothbrush. The topsoil of the pot should be clean and free of debris, and the plant must be accurately labeled with its proper name. Remember, too, that an entry not conforming to the specific classification as listed is disqualified.

The size of the blossoms should be in proportion to the shape of the plant and density of the foliage. A compact specimen and abundant bloom make for vital points.

With tuberous begonias, the depth and the form of the flower are prime considerations; the size of the bloom should not be too large or too small in relation to the plant foliage.

Leaf color must be clear and deep, without fading or yellowing of tones. In hairy-leaved begonias the foliage should glow. Plants that have a color overlay, like *B. sanguinea* and some Rex types, should show a distinction between the overlay and the basic leaf coloring. Begonias with heavy tomentum, like *B. incana* and *B. kellermanni,* should show color through the felt. The depth of color in alien markings is also important.

Fibrous begonias are more apt to be winners if they are tall and bushy, the foliage starting from the soil level on the stalk. Rhizomatous plants should be uniform in size, and all rhizomes should be contained within the pot.

A gigantic plant, although it may attract attention from the crowd, does not necessarily mean a winning plant. Size is only one aspect of the whole number of points recorded.

Grow and show. And good luck!

Photographing Begonias

When your begonias are at the peak of flower and form, you will want to preserve that moment. Photography becomes another enjoyable hobby. Not only is it satisfying to see your own plants on film; photographing also enables you to keep a progress record. Then it is an easy matter to look back and see exactly how much the plants are gaining in growth from year to year.

Today, new cameras and film make it possible for any person to take a picture. You don't have to be a professional to get a decent photograph. And color enlargements of your best plants are always splendid wall decoration for library or den.

To select your camera, first talk it over with a reputable dealer. Tell him what kind of pictures you want to take—

for reproduction, for color slides, close-ups—he will guide you accordingly. Most photographers prefer a high-quality single-lens reflex type of camera. You can look through the lens and see the subject in full color as well as the composition of the resulting photograph.

The quality of a photograph depends on many factors. These include lighting, focus, camera angle, correct exposure, and choice of background. A plain background is best for photographing plants; it allows leaves and flower parts to be the attraction rather than something behind the plant. Matboard from art stores comes in a variety of colors. For color photography blue and black sheets work the best for me. Black-and-white shots are more difficult because all parts of the plant and background are reproduced in tones of gray. Lighting is the secret here, and Experience the teacher.

If I want a portrait of a specimen plant, I photograph it indoors against a black corduroy background. I use floodlights at varying distance. Outdoors, I photograph with a light meter, occasionally with a supplementary flash. When I photograph a begonia, I take three shots—a close-up of the flower, a tight shot of foliage and flower, and a distant shot showing the pot and the plant. Select a camera angle that shows off the plant to the best advantage. Straight-on photography is usually uninteresting; avoid it. Experiment; take pictures from many different angles.

Indoors or out, a tripod is necessary for flower photography. It enables you to be free to arrange the subject taken, so you can get good composition and design.

APPENDIX

Where to Buy Begonias

Antonelli Brothers, 2545 Capitola Road, Santa Cruz, Calif. *Grand selection of tuberous begonias. Color catalog 25 cents.*

Barrington Greenhouses, 860 Clements Bridge Road, Barrington, N.J. *All types of plants available. Fine mail-order house.*

Green Hills Nursery, 2131 Vallejo Street, St. Helena, Calif. *All kinds of begonias.*

Logee's Greenhouses, 55 North Street, Danielson, Conn. *Excellent selection of all kinds of begonias. Color catalog, 25 cents.*

Karutz Greenhouses, Dept. B, 92 Chestnut Street, Wilmington, Mass. *Catalog, 25 cents. Fine selection of begonias.*

Paul P. Lowe, 23045 S. W. 123rd., Goulds, Fla. *Price list free. Begonias unlimited.*

Merry Gardens, Camden, Me. *Color catalog 50 cents. Large choice of over 200 begonias.*

Mrs. Bert Routh, Louisburg, Mo. *Price list 10 cents. Begonias and other house plants.*

Palos Verdes Begonia Farm, 4111 242nd Street, Walteria, Calif. *Complete selection of tuberous begonias. No price list available.*

Tropical Paradise Greenhouses, 8825 W. 79th Street, Overland Park, Kan. *Catalog 50 cents. Many fine new cultivars; large selection.*

The Begonia House, 2320 Coronet Place, Jackson, Miss. *Price list 10 cents. Over 300 begonias.*

Rudolph Ziesenhenne, 1130 Milpas Street, Santa Barbara, Calif. *Begonia seed.*

Vetterle and Reinelt, Capitola, Calif. *Color Catalog.* *Fine selection of tuberous begonias.*

Shipping Plants

Because begonias are not as readily available at growers as other plants, you might want to exchange plants with friends in other states. Some of my best stock has come this way. Bartering or trading within your state does not require a permit. However, if you wish to ship to other places, write to the Department of Agriculture of your state. Tell them what you want to do, and they will tell you whether you need a permit.

To ship cuttings, wrap a ball of moist sphagnum moss around the base of the plant. Cover with a square of aluminum foil held in place with a rubber band. Roll the begonia in a piece of newspaper and leave the top open so that air can reach the leaves. Then pack the cuttings right-side up and fill in and around with newspapers.

Mature begonias are best shipped in plastic pots. They weigh less. Make sure the soil is evenly moist; water it well the day before shipping. Insert a label into the soil at the edge of the pot. Put a protective layer of sphagnum moss over the soil and a square of aluminum foil over the pot and the soil, up to the stem of the plant. Secure it with a rubber band. Roll each begonia in several sheets of newspapers, and leave the top open. Place packages upright in the container and push crumpled papers into the empty spaces.

I find air parcel post the best way of shipping. It is somewhat expensive, but plants are usually delivered the day after shipment.

Begonias with Small Leaves

B. acuminata	B. fuchsiodes
B. alinifolia	'Lulandi'
B. cooperi	B. obscura
'Corbeille de Feu'	'Richmondensis'
'Digswelliana'	'Sachsen'

BEGONIAS WITH LARGE LEAVES

'Corallina de Lucerna'
'Fischer's Ricinifolia'
'Fuscomaculata'
B. *luxurians*
B. *manicata*

'Ricinifolia'
'Rubaiyat'
'Ricky Minter'
'Ross Swisher'
'Templini'

BEGONIAS FOR FOLIAGE

B. *acida*
B. *boweri*
B. *decora*
B. *goegoensis*
B. *griffithi*

B. *imperialis*
B. *metallica*
B. *manicata aureo-maculata*
B. *venosa*
All Rexes

BEGONIAS FOR FLOWER

B. *coccinea*
'Corallina de Lucerna'
'Ellen Dee'
B. *manicata*
B. *nitida*
'Orange Rubra'

'Pinafore'
'President Carnot'
Semperflorens varieties
Tuberous Begonias
'Weltoniensis'

BEGONIAS FOR SCENT

B. *foliosa*
B. *glaucophylla*
B. *hydrocotylifolia*

B. *nitida*
B. *roxburghi*

BEGONIAS FOR SUN

B. *fuchsioides*
B. *incana*
B. *nitida*
B. *kellermanni*
'Paul Bruant'

B. *odorata rosea*
B. *roxburghi*
'Templini'
'Thurstoni'
B. *venosa*

BEGONIAS FOR WARM LOCATIONS

B. *acida*
B. *acuminata*
B. *dichroa*
B. *goegoensis*

B. *heracleifolia*
'Margaritae'
B. *phyllmaniaca*
B. *venosa*

BEGONIAS FOR COOL LOCATIONS

B. *acuminata*
B. *convolvulacea*
B. *heracleifolia*
B. *hydrocotylifolia*
'Feasti'

B. *luxurians*
B. *manicata aureo-maculata*
'Mrs. Townsend'
B. *perfectifolia*
B. *roezli*

BIBLIOGRAPHY

BEGONIAS FOR AMERICAN HOMES AND GARDENS
Helen K. Krauss
The Macmillan Company, 1947
New York, N.Y.

BEGONIAS AND HOW TO GROW THEM
Bessie R. Buxton
Oxford University Press, 1946
New York, N.Y.

BUXTON CHECK LIST OF BEGONIAS
American Begonia Society, 1957
Los Angeles, California

1001 BEGONIA QUESTIONS
Edited by Elvin McDonald
Diversity Books, 1967
Kansas City, Mo.

SUCCESSFUL BEGONIA CULTURE
F. J. Bedson
Transatlantic Arts, 1954
Hollywood-by-the-Sea, Florida

TUBEROUS BEGONIAS
Worth Brown
M. Barrows and Company, 1948
New York, N.Y.

TUBEROUS ROOTED BEGONIAS AND THEIR CULTURE
George Otten
Dodd, Mead & Company, 1949
New York, N.Y.

INDEX

(Names of species are italics; cultivars are caps and single quotes)

Italic folios indicate illustrations

'A. D. Davis,' 94
'Albo Picta,' 103
'Alice,' 89
'Alleryi,' 16, 18, 66
'Aloha,' 64
'Alpha Gere,' 18; basket, 108; outdoors, 52
'Alto Scharff,' 66
'Altrincham Pink,' 110
'Alzasco,' 71
American Begonia Society, 34, 40, 113; *Bulletin*, 113
American Horticultural Council, 113
American Horticultural Society, 113
'Ami Jean Bard,' 58
'Andy,' 64
'Andy Lee,' 60
Angel Wing, 13, 15, 17, 18, 48, 50, 70-82; climate, 51, 52; containers for, 24; greenhouse, 44; humidity, 27; indoors, 41; pruning, 28; stem cuttings, 36
ants, 31, 32
aphids, 32
'Arabelle,' 74
'Argentea Guttata,' 71

'Arthur Mallet,' 80
'Aureola,' 96
'Autumn Glow,' 93
'Avila,' 96

'Baardse Glory,' 110
'Baardse Wonder,' 110
'Baby Rainbow,' 103
'Ballet,' 64
basket begonias, 15, 18, 104-108
'Bearded,' 96
'Beatrice Haddrell,' 83
B. acetosa, 83
B. acida, 120, 121
B. acontifolia, 50
B. acuminata, 16, 106, 119, 121
B. acutangularis, 71
B. albo-picta, 71
B. alnifolia, 20, 77, 119
B. aridicaulis, 97
B. barkeri, 50
B. boliviensis, 60
B. boweri (Eyelash), 13, 18, 97, 120; hybrid, 39; *major*, 97; *marga-nigra*, 97
B. bradei, 66
B. cathayana, 16, 74
B. cheimantha ("Busy Lizzie"), 44

B. chimborazo, 89
B. clarkei, 60
B. coccinea, 71, 72, 80, 120
B. conchaefolia, 15, 89
B. convolvulacea, 15, 50, 106, 121
B. cooperi, 119
B. crispula, 89
B. dayi, 89, 90
B. decora, 15, 84
B. dichroa, 71, 121
B. digswelliana, 45
B. dregei, 45, 98, *100,* 111
B. evansiana, 20
B. fernando costae, 66
B. fimbriata, 61
B. foliosa, 16, 18, 20, 45, 98, *100,* 120
B. froebeli, 61
B. fuchsiodes, 16, 45, 119, 120
B. fulgens, 61
B. glaucophylla, 120
B. goegoensis, 16, 84
B. griffithi, 16, 98, 120
B. hemsleyana, 86
B. heracleifolia, 15, 18, 86, 87, 121
B. hugelli, 66
B. hydrocotylifolia, 16, 98, 120, 121
B. imperialis (Otto Forster), 13, 86, 87, 120
B. incana, 16, 66, 116, 120
B. kellermanni, 46, 76, 77, 116, 120
B. kenworthyi, hybrid, 39
B. laeteviridea, 66
B. leptotricha, 68, *69*
B. lubbersi, 80, *81*
B. luxurians, 16, 66, *67,* 120, 121
B. maculata, 16, 73
B. manicata, 14, 120
B. manicata aureo-maculata, 86, 120, 121
B. masoniana, 82

B. mazae, 14, 89
B. metallica, 66, 120
B. micranthera, 61
B. nelumbifolia, 50
B. nigrans, 86
B. nitida, 16, 77, 120
B. obscura, 119
B. odorata, rosea, 120
B. parilis, 77, 78
B. pearcei, 61
B. perfectifolia, 121
B. phyllmaniaca, 121
B. picta, 61
B. popenoei, 50
B. purpurea, 86, *88*
B. richardsiana, 104
B. ricinifolia, 13
B. roezlii, 77, 121
B. rotundifolia, 98, *102*
B. roxburghi, 67, 120
B. sanguinea, 116
B. scandens, 50
B. sceptrum, 77, 78
B. scharffi (B. haageana), 67
B. schmidtiana, 77, *79*
B. serratipetala, 77
B. socotrana, 109, 111
B. squamosa, 90
B. strigillosa, 46, 89
B. sunderbruchii, 86
B. tomentosa, 77
B. valdensium, 77, 80
B. veitchi, 61
B. vellozoana, 89
B. venosa, 16, 20, 46, 68, *68,* 120, 121
B. ventura, 61
B. vitifolia, 46
'Bessie Buxton,' 83
'Black Diamond,' 93
'Black Knight,' 57, 58
'Bonanza,' 57, 58
bonemeal, 22
bonsai, 45
'Bo-Beep,' 64
botrytis, 31

'Bow Arriola,' 97
'Bow Chancee,' 97
'Bow Joe,' 97
'Bow Nigra,' 97
'Bronze King,' 96
'Brookes,' 74, 75
'Bunchi,' 15, 84
'Burvel,' 93

'Calico,' 93, 103
'Calla Queen,' 112
Camellia (ruffled), 57
Camelliaeflora, 56
'Can Can,' 18, 93
'Cardoza Gardens,' 93
'Carlton's Delight,' 64
'Carol Star,' 89
'Carolina,' 111
'Catalina,' 16, 80, *81*
'Chance,' 97
'Chantilly Lace,' 97, 99
charcoal, 28, 36, 37
'Charm,' 112
Cheimanthus, 15, 111
'Cherie,' 60
'Cherry Sundae,' 112
'Chiala Rosea,' 70
'China Boy,' 98
'China Doll,' 14, 18, 98
'Chinook,' 57, 58
'Cinderella,' 64
classification, 14, 15
climate, 51
'Comtesse Louise Erdody,' 96
'Congo,' 89
'Constance,' 73
containers, 23; outdoor, 52
'Copper Gold,' 58
'Corallina,' 16
'Corallina de Lucerna,' 106, 120
'Corbeille de Feu,' 16, *76*, 77, 119
'Crednerii,' 70
'Crestabruchi,' 20, 84
'Crimson Glow,' 96
Cristata, 56

cultivars, 19, 20
'Curly Carnot,' 93
'Curly Locks,' 64
'Curly Merry Christmas,' 96
'Curly Silver Sweet,' 96
'Cypraea,' 70

'Dainty Maid,' 64
'Dark Carnot,' 94
'Darlene,' 60
'D'Artagnon,' 106
'Decorus,' 71
Diadema, 92
dichroa, 39
'Di-Erna,' 71
'Digswelliana,' 77, 119
diseases, 29, 31; fungus, 27
dormancy, 29
'Douglas Nesbit,' 73
drafts, 93
'Drosti,' 70
'Dusky Rose,' 96

'Edith M.,' 89
'Ellen Dee,' 18, 106, 120
'Elsie M. Frey,' 16, 106, *107*
'Elvira Swisher,' 73
'Emily Clibran,' 110
'E. O. Orpet,' 108
'Ernest K.,' 64
'Erythrophylla' (beefsteak, Feasti), 18, 45, 84, 85; 'Helix,' 84
'Evergreen,' 96
exhibitions, 114
'Exquisite,' 110

'Fairy,' 110
'Fantasy,' 93
'Feasti,' 121
fertilizing, 26
fibrous: for exhibition, 114; rooted, 15
'Fiesta,' 93
Fimbriata: flower, 56
'Firefly,' 64

'Fischer's Ricinifolia,' 120
'Flambeau,' 58
'Flamboyante,' 58
'Florence Carrell,' 106
foliar feeding, 26
'Frances Powell,' 57, 58
'Frieda Grant,' 80
fuchsiodes, 39
'Fuscomaculata,' 84, 120

'Gaucho,' 57, 58
'Gigi Fleetham,' 73
'Gloire de Sceaux,' 111
'Glory of St. Albans,' 94
gravel bed, 27
greenhouse, 43
'Green Thimbleberry,' 64
'Grey Feather,' 72, 73

hanging basket, 59–60
heel cuttings, 38
Heimalis (Clibran), 109-111
'Helen Harms,' 58
'Helen Teupel,' 94
'Helen W. King,' 73
Hirsutes, 15, 18, 19, 24, 26, 65-
    70; characteristics of, 65; for
    exhibition, 114
humidifiers, 27
humidity, 27
'Huntington Lake,' 94
hybrids, 19
hybridizing, 38, 39
hygrometer, 27

'Illsley,' 89
'Illustrata,' 89, *90*
'Immense,' 14, 89
'Interlaken,' 73
Imperialis, 39
'Indra,' 108
insecticides, 29–33
insects: sucking, 31
'Ivy Ever,' 103

'Jack Horner,' 64
'Joe Hayden,' 50
'John C. Mensing,' 110

'Kathleyana,' 94
'King Edward IV,' 96

'Lady Clare,' 70
'Lady Mac,' 111
lamps: fluorescent, 41
lath house, 49
'Laura Eglebert,' 73
leaf: cuttings, 37; growth, 22;
    spot, 31
'Leo C. Shippy,' 13
'Leza,' 60
light, 21
'Limminghei,' 13, 16, 18, 106,
    108; outdoors, 52
'Lloydi Yellow,' 108
'Loma Alta,' 66
Lou-Anne, 60
'Louise Closson,' 98
'Lucerna,' 14
'Lucy Locket,' 64
'Lulandi,' 98, *101,* 119

'Mandarin,' 57, 58
manicata, 39
'Maphil' (Cleopatra), 50, 86, *88*
'Margaritae,' 15, 70, 121
Marginata: flower, 56
'Marie B. Holly,' 80
'Marietta,' 111
'Marina,' 111
'Marjorie Daw,' 108
'Marjorie Gibbs,' 111
mealybugs, 30, 32
'Medora,' 103
'Melisse,' 80
'Merry Christmas,' 94, *95*
metallica, 39
mildew, 31
Miniature, 15, 96-104
misting, 27, 48
miticide, 30

mixes, 22
'Mme. Fanny Giron,' 106
'Mme. Richard Galle,' 58
'Modesty,' 94
'Mountain Haze,' 96
'Mrs. Fred D. Scripps,' 18, 70
'Mrs. H. G. Moon,' 94
'Mrs. Townsend,' 121
Multifloras, 58

Narcissiflora: flower, 56
'Neely Gaddis,' 66
'Nellie Visset,' 111
nematodes, 31
'New Hampshire,' 64
nutrients, 22

'Oadi,' 77
'Oiai,' 94
'Orange Dainty,' 98
'Orange Parade,' 74, 75
'Orange Rubra,' 14, 106, 120
'Oregon Sunset,' 94
'Orient,' 96
'Othello,' 64
'Otto Forster,' 13
overwatering, 25

'Pacific Sunset,' 96
'Pansy,' 104
'Paul Bruant,' 120
'Peace,' 94
peat moss, 25
peat pot, 24, 25
perlite, 36
pests, 29, 32
'Peter Pan,' 94
'Phyllomaniaca,' 15, 82
Picotee: double, 57; flower, 56
'Pinafore,' 73, 120
'Pink Camellia,' 106
'Pink Parade,' 74
'Pink Perfection,' 111
'Pink Rubra,' 73
'Pink Shower,' 60
'Pink Spot Lucerne,' 73

'Pink Wave,' 73
'Pink Wonder,' 64
'Pistachio,' 65
'President Carnot,' 106, *109*, 120
'Prunifolia,' 70
pruning, 28

'Queen of Hanover,' 94
'Queen Wilhelmina,' 94

'Rambouillet,' 58
'Red Berry,' 98
'Red Compta,' 108
red spiders, 32
'Red Wing,' 98
repotting, 28
Rex, 13, 15, 18, 26, 48, 92-96, *95*, 120; climate, 51; containers, 24; dormancy, 29; for exhibition, 114; in greenhouse, 44; humidity, 27; leaf cuttings, 37
Rhizomatous, 13, 15, 18, 19, 48, 50, 82-90; climate, 51; containers, 24; cuttings, 37, 38; for exhibition, 115; in greenhouse, 44; humidity, 27; repotting, 28; outdoors, 52
'Richmondensis,' 119
'Ricinifolia,' 18, 82, 86, 120
'Ricky Minter,' 13, 14, 90, *91*, 120
'Robinson Peach,' 74
'Romance,' 74
roots: development, 22; hormone powder, 36; nematodes, 32
'Rosada,' 57, 58
'Rosa Kugel,' 98
'Rosalind,' 111
'Rosea-Gigantea,' 82
Rose form, flower, 56
'Rose Queen,' 111
'Ross Swisher,' 120
'Royal Flush,' 57, 58

'Rubaiyat,' 74, 120
'Ruby Jewel,' 112
'Rufida,' 67
'Ruth Anne,' 82

'Sachsen,' 119
'Saga,' 65
'Salamander,' 94
sand, 36
'Sara-Belle,' 74
scale insects, 30, 32
'Scarlet O'Hara,' 96
Scope, 31, 32
seed, 35, 36
Semperflorens, 13-15, 24, 63-65;
    Calla-lily type, 111, 112; cli-
    mate, 51; humidity, 27; hy-
    brids, 39; outdoors, 52; prun-
    ing, 29; stem cuttings, 36;
    varieties, 120; wax, 63
'Shasta,' 74
'Shippy's Garland,' 108
'Silver Fleece,' 96
'Silver King,' 94
'Silver Song,' 73
'Sir Percy,' 90
'Skeezar,' 13, 50, 86
slugs, 31, 32
snails, 31, 32
'Snowdrop,' 111
soil, 21, 22; packaged, 23
soil formulas for: fibrous, 22;
    Rex, 23; Rhizomatous, 22
'Solid Silver,' 94
South America, 82
'South Pacific,' 65
'Spaulding,' 90, *91*
species, 19
'Speculata,' 90, *91*
sphagnum moss, 35, 119
'Spirit of Norway,' 111
'Spring Song,' 73
'Star Bright,' 98
'Stardust,' 94
stem and root rot, 31
stem cuttings, 36

'Sunburst,' 96
'Swanson's Pink,' 65
'Sweet Home,' 59
'Sylvan Grandeur,' 73

'Tasso,' 59
temperature, 27
'Templini,' 120
terrarium planting, 46, 47
thrips, 32
'Thrush,' 94
'Thurstoni,' 120
time of bloom, 15
'Tove,' 111
trailing, 13; pruning, 29
tree form, 46
Tuberhybrida, 54
tuberous, 13, 15, 58, *59*, 120;
    Calla-lily type, 51, 52; cane-
    type, 50, 51; climate, 51, 52;
    flower forms, 56, 57; in gar-
    den beds, 61; as gifts, 44;
    outdoors, 48, 54; pinching,
    29; propagation, 61; species,
    60; watering, 54

'Vander Meer's Glorie,' 111
'Vedderi,' 70
'Velma,' 74
vermiculite, 35, 36
'Vernon,' 65
'Vesperia,' 70
'Viaude,' 68, *69*
'Viau-Scharff,' 68
'Virbob,' 104

watering, 25
'Weltoniensis,' 16, 18, 82, 120
'Westport Beauty,' 65
white flies, 32
Wild Rose, 60
window boxes, 53, 54
'Winkie,' 65
'Winter Jewel' *(bartonea)*, 103
'Winter Queen,' 94
'Wooly Bear,' 68, *69*